AMAZING PEACE

THROUGH THE STORMS OF LIFE

*How to Find and Keep
the Peace of God
in Those Uncertain
Moments of Our Lives*

GEORGE FOSTER

I COMMEND TO YOU GEORGE FOSTER, a friend of mine for a quarter of a century, a gentle giant, a leader in missions, an author, speaker, and a man of God.

He writes from his personal experiences, opening practical yet interesting modern windows of understanding on ancient truths of God's Word. I loved his true stories and stayed interested until the end.

George leads the reader to Jesus, our safe haven in every storm, the "author and finisher of our faith," and the "Prince of Peace."

Read, apply, and enjoy! I did.

LOREN CUNNINGHAM
Founder, Youth with a Mission
President, University of the Nations

IN A UNIQUE WAY, REV. GEORGE FOSTER HAS LAID DOWN STEPS TO EXPERIENCE GOD'S PEACE. You will find the presentation refreshing and very practical. We can follow the steps for ourselves and once more experience God's peace. Or we can share these steps with someone who desperately needs this peace of God in the midst of the confusion, stress, and anxiety of the everyday world.

I have had the privilege to work with Rev. George Foster many times. He has always been a blessing to me and to all to whom he ministers. He has written many other books that have been a great help to many. *Amazing Peace Through the Storms of Life* will help you in your personal relationship with God. I highly recommend this book to you and to your friends.

ROBERT R. CUNVILLE
Associate Evangelist
Billy Graham Evangelistic Association

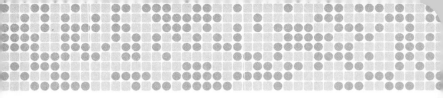

TABLE OF CONTENTS

1. WHEN THE STORMS OF LIFE ARE RAGING............. 11

2. MAKE A CHOICE TO REJOICE!........................ 27

3. MAKE UP YOUR MIND TO BE KIND........................... 43

4. DON'T SWEAT. DON'T FRET.
   DON'T GET UPSET.. 59

5. MAKE A WAY TO PRAY EVERY DAY 81

6. MAKE GRATITUDE YOUR ATTITUDE 101

7. LET HIGHER THINKING KEEP YOU
   FROM SINKING... 123

8. DON'T LOSE IT. DON'T ABUSE IT.
   DON'T FAIL TO USE IT!....................................... 143

9. INCREASE YOUR PEACE.................................... 159

APPENDIX: GOD WILL ESTABLISH HIS
   KINGDOM OF PEACE 175

TO
DOLLY

She made a huge impact on me the first time
I saw her. Tall and slender, she had big blue eyes and
dimples that made their appearance every time
she smiled, and she smiled most of the time!
It was her joy—the likes of which I have never seen
elsewhere before or since—that impressed me most.
She also has a rare ability to empathize with people in
their joys and sorrows. Like no one else I know,
she weeps with those who weep and rejoices with
those who rejoice. She's given lots of compassionate
hugs and smiles, and she's shed lots of heartfelt tears.
She's had her own share of heartaches along the way,
but whether despite them or because of them, she has
learned to model what I share in these pages.
I've gained understanding from her.
My wife since September 12, 1964,
it's to Dolly that this book is lovingly dedicated.

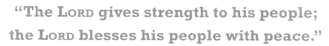

"The Lord gives strength to his people;
the Lord blesses his people with peace."

PSALM 29:11

. . . .

"Mightier than the thunder
of the great waters,
mightier than the breakers
of the sea—
the Lord on high is mighty."

PSALM 93:4

"PEACE
I LEAVE
WITH YOU."

JOHN 14:27

WHEN THE STORMS
OF LIFE ARE RAGING

A CONTEST WAS HELD and a prize offered to the painter who could best depict on canvas a feeling of peace.

As expected, dozens of artists submitted beautiful rural scenes painted in soft pastel tones.

To everyone's surprise, however, the winning entry was painted by an artist who used bold, dark strokes to portray a violent storm with fierce wind, driving rain, and jagged lightning. Lines converged on a cleft in an enormous rock where—protected from the elements and completely undisturbed—perched a bright, irrepressible bird.

Isn't that the peace we need? In fast-moving and threatening times like these, what good is a peace that demands a controlled environment where everything goes our way? We need a peace of heart and mind to see us through the storm when our environment goes berserk. It can't be the false peace that comes from ignoring or denying the existence of trouble. We need a peace that enables us to look trouble in the face and embrace life with confidence, strength, and joy.

JESUS TAKES US INTO THE STORM

After the terrible terrorist attacks of September 11, 2001, people were asking, "Where is God; doesn't He care about us?" I was reminded of the storm that assailed Jesus and His disciples on the Sea of Galilee, causing the disciples to cry, "Don't you care if we die?" Here's the story as the Bible relates it in Mark 4:35–5:1:

> *"That day when evening came, he said to his disciples,*
> *'Let us go over to the other side.'*
>
> *Leaving the crowd behind, they took him along, just as he was, in the boat. There were also other boats with him. A furious squall came up, and the waves broke over the boat, so that it was nearly swamped.*
>
> *Jesus was in the stern, sleeping on a cushion. The disciples*

woke him and said to him, 'Teacher, don't you care if we drown?'

He got up, rebuked the wind and said to the waves, 'Quiet! Be still!' Then the wind died down and it was completely calm. He said to his disciples, 'Why are you so afraid? Do you still have no faith?'

They were terrified and asked each other, 'Who is this? Even the wind and the waves obey him!'

They went across the lake to the region of the Gerasenes."

Reading how Jesus calmed the storm and took the disciples safely to the other side, I was awed by His power and authority— but I also had to ask: Why did He take them *into* the storm? Why does He take *us* into storms?

As I asked myself that question, I remembered a storm I had gone through not in a boat, but in a small plane. As we approached the runway to land in the world-class city of Curitiba, Paraná state, Brazil, we were buffeted by a hailstorm and powerful winds. Unable to land, we were forced to endure the storm for what seemed like an eternity. The passenger on my left sat motionless, gripping the armrests. Across the aisle a passenger perspired profusely from the forehead. Children began to laugh and then cry. Many of the plastic bags for motion sickness were put to use. The pilot could not run from the storm; he had to face it head-on. After taking a beating for several minutes, the pilot flew the plane to another city to wait out the storm.

When we landed, a flight attendant made this announcement: "Please remain seated. The storm will pass by quickly, and we will return to Curitiba."

Those words were not as comforting as she meant them to be. Upon hearing them, a fellow passenger announced what many of us were thinking: "Either you open the doors to this plane, or I will!" We all gathered at the front of the plane, discovering that the hailstones had removed most of the paint from the leading edge of the wings.

We waited about thirty minutes and reentered the plane, each passenger receiving two motion-sickness bags at the door—but the flight back was uneventful. I was thankful I didn't need the bags, but I confess that I was weak-kneed. Finally landing at our destination, the passengers exclaimed almost as one voice, "We've been born again!"

Why did Jesus take me into that storm? Why does He take *you* into storms? Why do we go through such stressful, painful, and threatening moments in our lives? I realized that many of the unpleasant situations we experience are of our own making or the result of others' mistakes. "A man reaps what he sows" and sometimes reaps the results of other people's sowing, as well. Sometimes we get into trouble and there is no one to blame. God allows it for certain reasons yet to be discovered. Let me suggest five possible reasons:

JESUS TAKES US INTO THE STORM SO WE WILL CALL UPON HIM. Several disciples were professional fishermen, but they were not prepared for such a gale. They could not rely on their ability or experience for survival. They had to depend upon Jesus. As the disciples found, storms shake us out of our complacency, strip us of self-sufficiency, and draw us closer to Jesus where we can acknowledge our need and ask for His help in our distress.

Most of us have a sense that the only things that are truly safe are the things we place in God's caring hands. The disciples were not worried about their fishing tackle; they were concerned for their lives. The storms we face are often the means God uses to get our attention and bring about the most important transfer we can make—the transfer of the care and control of our lives to Him.

JESUS TAKES US INTO THE STORM TO GROW OUR FAITH. I've observed that faith grows in four principle environments: when it's nourished, when it's activated, when it's tested, and when it's rewarded. We don't always feed our faith or activate it as we should, so God puts it to the test:

> *"These [trials] have come so that your faith—of greater worth than gold, which perishes even though refined by fire—may be proved genuine and may result in praise, glory and honor when Jesus Christ is revealed"* (1 PETER 1:7).

My friend Carlos planted a tree in southern Brazil. To protect it from the strong *Minuano* winds that blow there, he built a wooden shelter around it. He watered the tree and protected it but, despite all the care he gave it, the tree did not grow as he expected. When he gave up and dismantled the shelter, the unprotected tree began to grow. The wind forced the tree to extend its fingerlike roots deeper into the soil, where it found the nourishment it needed to develop as it should.

Many times it's like that with us. When our faith is tested, we are forced to feed and activate it as we might not otherwise do. As we "dig in" and "hold on" to Christ, our faith grows. That motivates us to feed and activate it again and again, and it is rewarded with God's providence and provisions time after time. The cycle repeats itself endlessly.

JESUS TAKES US INTO THE STORM TO BUILD OUR CHARACTER AND PREPARE US FOR GREATER CHALLENGES. We face trouble from a variety of sources: from ourselves, from others, from living in a fallen world, and from Satan. God sometimes allows problems to come from several sources all at once—but always with a purpose as James 1:3–4 says:

> *"The testing of your faith develops perseverance. Perseverance must finish its work so that you may be mature and complete, not lacking anything."*

There was a time when I felt as if everything in my life was going wrong. Complaining to God, I felt an urge to read Jeremiah 12, where I discovered that the prophet was complaining for the same reasons I was. He knew he would not win an argument with God, but in verse 1 he said:

> *"You are always righteous, O Lord, when I bring a case before you. Yet I would speak with you about your justice: Why does the way of the wicked prosper? Why do all the faithless live at ease?"*

I don't know what Jeremiah expected to hear—certainly not what God said to him in verse 5:

> " 'If you have raced with men on foot and they have worn you out, how can you compete with horses? If you stumble in safe country, how will you manage in the thickets by the Jordan?' "

These words disappointed me because I felt that God was speaking to me; however, it wasn't what I wanted to hear. I wanted words of hope, assurance, and comfort. What I found was a warning that things could get worse!

Later, as I read the text again, I recognized that God was with me and would help me through any situation I faced—if I would trust Him, allow Him to strengthen me, and faithfully do what He called me to do.

A few weeks later, my friend Jim Stier, former international chairman of Youth with a Mission (YWAM), shared that he, too, had gone through severe trials and that the Lord had spoken to him through the same verses. We were comforted by the understanding that our character was being forged on the anvil of the difficult experiences we were facing and that if we remained faithfully committed to God's purposes

for us, we would be well prepared to face whatever
might come in the future.

JESUS TAKES US INTO THE STORM SO WE
MAY HELP OTHERS THROUGH THEIR STORMS.
When our five-day-old baby died, we received letters from
several concerned and compassionate friends, but the most
comforting of all the letters came from two different women
who had also lost babies and wrote from personal experience.
That showed us that trials prepare us as nothing else can to
help those who go through similar experiences.

Paul wrote to a suffering church about the "Father of
compassion and the God of all comfort, who comforts us in
all our troubles, so that we can comfort those in any trouble
with the comfort we ourselves have received from God"
(2 Corinthians 1:3–4). Our pain brings God's comfort and
compassion, which we in turn pass on to others in their pain.

In our case, our string of trials ran for several months until
one afternoon when Dolly and I were faced with another
one—another surgery—and we felt what I sometimes call
a "holy revolt" that drove us to a moment when we took a stand.
We decided to pray and trust God for a miraculous healing that
not only solved her problem but ended the streak of afflictions

we had faced. It was like the moment when Jesus rose up in the boat and said, "Peace, be still" (Mark 4:39 KJV).

JESUS TAKES US INTO THE STORM TO REVEAL WHO HE IS AND WHAT HE CAN DO. When Jesus spoke to the winds and the waves, they became calm again. His control over the elements turned the disciples' fear into amazement and revealed something about Himself that they had never seen before.

We, too, will see amazing displays of His power in the midst of the most difficult problems we face—if we endure in faith until the answer comes. Of course we pray for the quick fix, but if the solution lingers, we must not give up hope! A delay is not a denial and does not mean that God will fail to meet our needs. If we wait trusting on God and obey what He tells us to do, we will hear Him say, "Peace! Be still!"

For these reasons and many more, followers of Jesus Christ are not exempt from the difficulties and trials of life. The Bible prepares us for them with the words "A righteous man may have many troubles" and promises, "but the LORD delivers him from them all" (Psalm 34:19). Jesus does not guarantee an easy journey at sea, but He promises a safe arrival on the shore. When we set our sights on His promise to take us safely

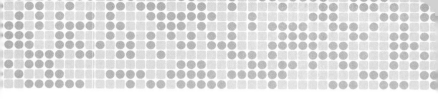

through our troubles, we will find the courage and strength we need while He guides us through the storm.

THE DISCIPLES AND
THEIR GREATEST STORM

The worst storm the disciples experienced was not the one on the Sea of Galilee, but the one that came to them just before the Lord's capture and horrific death at Calvary. Jesus knew that they would not face the storm but instead flee from it. Therefore, He warned them:

"A time is coming, and has come, when you will be scattered, each to his own home. You will leave me all alone. Yet I am not alone, for my Father is with me. I have told you these things, so that in me you may have peace. In this world you will have trouble. But take heart! I have overcome the world" (JOHN 16:32–33).

They would scatter, but Jesus would gather them again. They would have troubles, but Jesus would bring them peace. Tenderly, He reinforced what He had previously assured them, "Peace I leave with you; my peace I give you." Though He knew they would be severely tested and even fail, He completed His message by saying, "Do not let your hearts be troubled and do not be afraid" (John 14:27).

THE APOSTLE OF PEACE

Paul's life as an apostle was punctuated with problems, which he describes in painful yet hopeful words: "We are…hard pressed on every side, but not crushed; perplexed, but not in despair; persecuted, but not abandoned; struck down, but not destroyed" (2 Corinthians 4:8–9).

Paul's was not an easy life, but it was the life God had chosen for him. By embracing it he learned more about inner peace than if everything had gone his way. His was not the peace of the controlled environment. His was the peace in the midst of the storm. Paul's trials taught him patience, perspective, perseverance, and—through it all—peace.

To Paul, peace was a high-priority subject. He often greeted fellow believers with phrases such as, "Grace and peace to you from God our Father and the Lord Jesus Christ" (Philippians 1:2). He taught them to "make every effort to keep the unity of the Spirit through the bond of peace" (Ephesians 4:3). He stressed that Christ's kingdom is "righteousness, peace, and joy in the Holy Spirit" (Romans 14:17). He insisted that, "God is not a God of disorder but of peace" (1 Corinthians 14:33). His converts learned, "Let the peace of Christ rule in your hearts" (Colossians 3:15). He blessed Timothy: "May the Lord of peace himself give you peace at all times and in every way" (2 Thessalonians 3:16).

TAKING PEACE TO ANOTHER LEVEL

But of all of Paul's references to peace, it's in the book of Philippians (4:7) that Paul speaks about peace at its highest level—peace "which transcends all understanding"—a peace that guards the heart and mind when we are facing such adversity that, humanly speaking, there is no reason to be peaceful.

What's so impressive is that Paul wrote from the confines of a Roman prison—hardly a peaceful environment, but an environment that gives him high credibility to address the subject. From his experience of peace in troubled times, we can learn to experience God's peace in the difficult moments of our lives. The well-known passage Philippians 4:4–9 gives us clear steps to follow:

> *"Rejoice in the Lord always. I will say it again: Rejoice!*
> *Let your gentleness be evident to all. The Lord is near.*
> *Do not be anxious about anything, but in everything,*

by prayer and petition, with thanksgiving, present your
requests to God.

And the peace of God, which transcends all understanding,
will guard your hearts and your minds in Christ Jesus.

Finally, brothers, whatever is true, whatever is noble,
whatever is right, whatever is pure, whatever is lovely,
whatever is admirable—if anything is excellent or
praiseworthy—think about such things.

Whatever you have learned or received or heard from
me, or seen in me—put it into practice.

And the God of peace will be with you."

I often refer to this passage as "God's Prescription for Peace." Simple and succinct, it's the inspiration for everything I've written in this book. These verses correspond with the chapters in *Amazing Peace Through the Storms of Life.* The "prescription" is easy to understand but admittedly not easy to follow during hardships. Yet if we follow these guidelines, we have the double promise that the peace of God will guard us and the God of peace will be with us. The more we put it into practice, the more peace we will have.

THE CHALLENGES WE FACE

What are we like when the storms of life are raging? When our expectations are unfulfilled? When our dreams seem out of reach? When we feel that everything we counted on in our life is being shaken and we wonder what will remain? Do we have the peace of Jesus in the midst of the storm? Do we believe that Jesus will take us through? Can we rejoice? Can we be gentle? Can we win over anxiety? Can we pray and give thanks? Can we keep our thoughts healthy and uplifting? Can we walk the talk? Can we experience peace?

When I started writing about these things, my life was very peaceful. As I got further into the project, I faced a storm that brought me discomfort and forced me to take seriously the words I was writing and apply them daily.

The first step was to get a fresh perspective by resisting the urge to complain and instead making a commitment to rejoice.

"REJOICE
IN THE
LORD ALWAYS.
I WILL SAY IT AGAIN:
REJOICE!"

PHILIPPIANS 4:4

MAKE A CHOICE
TO REJOICE!

"I'VE GOT THE JOY, JOY, JOY, JOY, down in my heart." When we sang this upbeat song as a family the other night, I couldn't help wondering if it wasn't a defiantly joyful song like the one Paul and Silas sang when an earthquake shook their prison, opened their doors, and broke their chains.

Paul loved to write about joy. In Philippians alone, he used the word *joy* six times and *rejoice* eight times. Sometimes it was to say that he was rejoicing in spite of his difficulties—and sometimes it was to say that we should rejoice in spite of ours!

Inspired by Paul's joyful words, Charles Wesley wrote this classic hymn:

Rejoice, the Lord is King!
Your Lord and King adore;
Rejoice, give thanks, and sing,
And triumph evermore.
Lift up your heart,
Lift up your voice;
Rejoice, again, I say, rejoice.[1]

Though centuries apart in time and style, both songs are true to the spirit of God's Word: "Sing to him…. Let the hearts of those who seek the LORD rejoice" (1 Chronicles 16:9–10). It's amazing how music helps us to express joy when we feel it and recapture joy when we've lost it!

Years ago, our family returned to the United States from a time of overseas service. In need of refreshing, we went to a lively church and sang, "Put on a garment of praise for the spirit of heaviness." As we absorbed the energy of the music, the people, and the Holy Spirit, we felt joy and refreshment immediately.

More recently, when Dolly and I first visited the church we now attend, we were thrilled to join with the congregation in singing some of the classic hymns we love. We had been singing mostly contemporary songs—some wonderful, some not so wonderful—and returning to the hymns was like a homecoming for us. We were surprised to discover that we were choked with emotion and had tears running down our faces. At the close of the service, when we met the pastor for the first time, he said, "Wow! You really love those hymns." (Many would have just the opposite experience. They would express their joy by singing contemporary music rather than the classical hymns that are culturally removed from their experience.)

More dramatic than our experience, though, was that of a Chinese church leader who was placed in a concentration camp and assigned the daily job of cleaning the community cesspool. At first he resented such despicable treatment but soon realized that he was the only one in the camp who had time to be alone with God. He began to consider the cesspool a special place and started each day by singing, "I come to the garden alone." Imagine what it meant in that solitary pit to sing, "He walks with me and He talks with me and He tells me that I am His own. And the joy we share as we tarry there, none other has ever known."[2]

HERE'S THE TRUTH:

Everyone needs joy!

Every person wants it!

Jesus prayed that we would have it.

Paul told us how to get it.

Psalm 98:4 (KJV) exhorts, "Make a joyful noise unto the LORD."

James advised, "Count it all joy when you fall into various trials" (James 1:2 NKJV).

Joy is found in Jesus when we rejoice in Him.

We can rejoice our way to joy!

WHAT IS JOY?

Christians know that joy is more than a feeling or an on-again, off-again sentiment that changes according to the circumstances we face. Followers of Jesus Christ distinguish between lasting joy and situational happiness. Fun and joy are not necessarily synonymous. We believe that we can experience inner joy with no special external stimulus to make us happy.

Joy is positive posture, love of living, commitment to cheerfulness, and exuberance about life—no matter what life brings to us. Joy is a fruit that grows when the Holy Spirit fills us. We cultivate it by surrendering to Christ, embracing His will, trusting in His commitments to us, and rejoicing. More a choice than a feeling, more an attitude than a mood—joy is both a result of being with God and a reason for seeking Him.

David, when repenting of a terrible evil that had interrupted his fellowship with God, prayed that his sin would be forgiven, his heart would be cleansed, his spirit would be strengthened, and his joy would be restored (Psalm 51). He knew where to find joy: "You will fill me with joy in your presence, with eternal pleasures at your right hand" (Psalm 16:11). We experience true joy when we're in God's presence and have God as our one reliable source.

When the Bible says "rejoice," it's not merely telling us how we ought to feel. God tells us what to do, what not to do, what to say, what attitude to take, and even what to think about, but, because feelings are involuntary reactions, God does not say, "Feel joy." He says, *"Rejoice!"* If we have a personal relationship with God, we can rejoice when we feel joy, rejoice when we don't feel joy, and rejoice until we feel joy again. Rejoicing is our express route to joy.

A TIME TO GRIEVE, A TIME TO REJOICE

There are, of course, times to grieve. "A time to weep and a time to laugh, a time to mourn and a time to dance," says Ecclesiastes 3:4. We should neither deny that we grieve nor feel condemned when we do. Jesus, as He prepared to face the cross, confessed, " 'My soul is overwhelmed with sorrow to the point of death' " (Matthew 26:38). Jesus is called "a man of sorrows, and acquainted with grief" (Isaiah 53:3 KJV). Yet Jesus looked beyond his sorrow and "for the joy set before him endured the cross, scorning its shame, and sat down at the right hand of the throne of God" (Hebrews 12:2).

As Christians, we have resources that allow us to move from sorrow to joy. Our grief is not the hopeless sorrow of those who have no faith in Christ.

I saw this in Albania after the death of a young missionary named Paul. Paul had met and married Valbona, a lovely young Albanian woman, the only Christian in a Muslim family. Paul died at age thirty-four, leaving Valbona with two small children.

We joined with Valbona's family in mourning Paul's death until the moment when Paul's Christian friends wanted to celebrate his life and the eternal life we know in Christ. At the end of our time together, a young Muslim approached me and said, "When this is all over, I want to study the Bible. You Christians have a beautiful way of turning sorrow into joy."

There is a time to grieve and a time to stop grieving. When Israel was rebuilding Jerusalem, a day was chosen for an overdue public reading of God's Word. As the text was read, many began to weep. At that moment, Ezra, Nehemiah, and the Levites told them, "Go and enjoy choice food and sweet drinks, and send some to those who have nothing prepared. This day is sacred to our Lord. Do not grieve, for the joy of the LORD is your strength" (Nehemiah 8:10).

Turn your grief into joy and your joy into strength was the message of Nehemiah. In a similar way, Jesus encouraged His disciples: "You will grieve, but your grief will turn to joy" (John 16:20).

LAUGHTER OR JOY?

In the movie *Mary Poppins*, Dick van Dyke sang, "I love to laugh, long and loud and clear." We all do! And we love to have people laugh with us. "Laughter," goes the saying, "is the best medicine." Laughter is a stress reliever given to us by God. We should pay heed to Proverbs 17:22: "A cheerful heart is good medicine, but a crushed spirit dries up the bones."

This verse should have been read at a church where I went to speak one evening. It seemed strange that the men sat on one side of the building and the women on the other—and especially strange because they had asked me to speak on family life! The arrangement troubled me. The only advantage was that I could address the men as men and the women as women and look directly at them as I did.

What troubled me more than the seating arrangement was the fact that no one smiled! The people looked stern. The women had their hair pulled back so tightly that they would never need a face-lift—no matter what their age! I decided that if I accomplished nothing else that night, I had to make them laugh at least once. It took awhile, but they finally risked a few chuckles. I concluded that their lack of joy was due to the erroneous idea that one needed to be extremely serious to be accepted by God.

Abraham and Sarah would have disagreed with that idea. "Abraham was a hundred years old when his son Isaac was born to him. Sarah said, 'God has brought me laughter, and everyone who hears about this will laugh with me' " (Genesis 21:5–6).

David wouldn't have liked the somber church either. He wrote, "When the LORD brought back the captives to Zion, we were like men who dreamed. Our mouths were filled with laughter, our tongues with songs of joy" (Psalm 126:1–2).

Laughter is wonderful—certainly more desirable than the somber spirituality of the church I described—but it can also be a cover for inner sadness and a substitute for real joy. Some who laugh loudest are, as the song says, "laughing on the outside, crying on the inside."

A Reader's Digest article about Lucille Ball stated, "The sharpest humor springs not from funny things, but from such complex sources as emotional deprivation, anger, humiliation, and envy. Like so many of her fellow comedians, Lucy was deeply unhappy even as she made jokes on the air."

Joel Osteen tells of another humorist who brought laughter to large crowds but lacked joy himself. Feeling of little value, he went to a doctor, who suggested that he cheer up by attending a performance of the famous comedian in town. "But, Doctor," he answered sadly, "I am the comedian."

Feelings can be deceptive. How should we handle them? What significance should we attach to them? The verses that follow tell us that if we want to keep our feelings from deceiving and defeating us, we must make some tough choices in our lives. We must trust God to keep our feelings under His control. We must make a choice to rejoice, and we must do it constantly. We must do it with the confidence that God will use our choice and release to us the feelings that we need. Feelings go where our thoughts and choices take them.

FEELINGS

Good ones, bad ones, happy ones, sad ones...
Wouldn't it be nice if we only had glad ones!
But we don't.

They're sometimes uplifting, sometimes depressing,
One day joyful, one day distressing.

Tears mixed with laughter, joy mixed with pain,
We can't always control them or even explain.
Like spices, they vary. They give life its flavor.
They help us stand firm. They cause us to waver.

They're always with us. We can't live without them.
The question is: What will we do about them?
Neglect them? Reject them? Subject them? Direct them?
Too often we coddle, too often we dissect them.

It's only by thinking God's thoughts every day,
By saying the words God wants us to say,
By doing the things God wants us to do,
By choosing when choosing is the hard thing to do...

...That our feelings are conquered. They learn to obey
The tough choices we make as we live day by day.
Old habits give place to new ones that heal.
We're sustained by the One who designed us to feel.[3]

SO MANY CHOICES!

Do you tire of making choices? Do you wonder why
spiritual fruit can't grow with less effort? Like other fruit, it
must be cultivated. God's power is in us, but we only release
it when we believe God and make right choices.

In 2 Peter 1:3, 5–7, Peter writes:

> *"His divine power has given us everything we need for
> life and godliness through our knowledge of him who called
> us by his own glory and goodness.... For this very reason,
> make every effort to add to your faith goodness; and to goodness,
> knowledge; and to knowledge, self-control; and to self-control,
> perseverance; and to perseverance, godliness; and to godliness,
> brotherly kindness; and to brotherly kindness, love."*

Choices are not a substitute for grace; they are a means to grace. Author Larry Christenson explains the connection between our choices and God's grace and power in us:

> *"Think of the wooden forms that a carpenter builds before cement is poured. The forms describe the shape that the cement will take. When the cement hardens they will be thrown away; only the cement will endure. The form represents the believer's role. We do not work patience, kindness, or love into ourselves. We simply construct the outward form into which God pours His enduring work of holiness."* [4]

We make the choice to rejoice. God brings the joy!

MAKING A DAILY CHOICE TO REJOICE

Dolly's mother, Ruth Haase, was a joyful person who taught joy to her children. Part of the process was to ask them nearly every morning, "What day is it today?"

Her children usually became evasive when she asked, naming the day of the week or month or anything else. To each answer Ruth playfully replied, "That's not what I want to hear."

When Dolly and her siblings could think of nothing else to say, they would give Ruth the answer she was waiting for: "This is the day that the Lord has made. We will rejoice and be glad in it" (see Psalm 118:24). Ruth emphasized *"we will"* and made it a constant practice.

Dolly learned well. Her joy infects people from many nations. A treasured photo shows her hugging and jumping with teenaged girls in Kosovo while they all chanted, "It's going to get better! It's going to get better!" Because Dolly is a spontaneous person, some observers might think her joy comes without effort, but, like all of us, Dolly has to choose joy in the morning and throughout the day. I'm glad she does!

NOT JUST REJOICING— REJOICING IN THE LORD!

Paul did not say that he liked the color of his cell, the fit of his chains, or the smell of his guards. He rejoiced in God, in God's presence, in God's promises, in God's power, and in God's peace. He rejoiced *"in the Lord"*! It can happen only when we place all our faith in the Lord.

Joy comes when we cultivate and recognize the presence of Jesus and believe that He will either release us from our afflictions or sustain us through them and will use those afflictions to accomplish His purposes in our lives.

In troubled times we can take our cue from Paul, who was "sorrowful, yet always rejoicing" (2 Corinthians 6:10).

Or Jesus: " 'Blessed are you when men hate you, when they exclude you and insult you and reject your name as evil, because of the Son of Man. Rejoice in that day and leap for joy, because great is your reward in heaven' " (Luke 6:22–23).

Or James: "Consider it pure joy, my brothers, whenever you face trials of many kinds, because you know that the testing of your faith develops perseverance" (James 1:2–3).

Or Peter: "Rejoice that you participate in the sufferings of Christ, so that you may be overjoyed when his glory is revealed" (1 Peter 4:13).

Or Habakkuk: "Though the fig tree does not bud and there are no grapes on the vines, though the olive crop fails and the fields produce no food, though there are no sheep in the pen and no cattle in the stalls, yet I will rejoice in the LORD, I will be joyful in God my Savior" (Habakkuk 3:17–18).

REJOICING—EVEN IN THE MIDST OF PAIN

When my friend Ken goes to church, he likes to punctuate the sermon with words like "Amen! Praise God! Hallelujah!" No one ever has to ask if Ken was there! If he missed a service, everyone would miss his exclamations.

Yet Ken's joy, which touches so many people around him, is expressed despite the fact that he has constant pain in several parts of his body. He has had knee, hip, and shoulder replacements. His neck is fused to relieve pain. (He wishes it did.) However, if you ask him how he is, he answers, "God is good!" And Ken makes those around him feel good, too!

My friend Ray has back pain that limits his activity. Yet he writes, "Choose joy! Joy is a choice. Joy is a witness. Joy is a therapy. Joy is a habit. If Jesus, who drank so deeply of the world's sorrow, could be filled with so much fun and laughter, then so can I."

Abraham Lincoln had a way of making profound observations in uncomplicated ways. He said, "Most folks are about as happy as they make up their minds to be."

It takes energy, determination, and perseverance, but we can choose joy. We do it by replacing our thoughts and feelings of discouragement with hope, our fear with faith, our anger with forgiveness, and our resentment with words and songs of rejoicing. "Rejoice," says Paul. "Rejoice! Rejoice! Rejoice!"

Rejoicing in the Lord will put us in the right frame of mind to take the next step in Paul's pathway to peace....

"LET YOUR GENTLENESS BE EVIDENT TO ALL. THE LORD IS NEAR."

PHILIPPIANS 4:5

MAKE UP YOUR
MIND TO BE KIND

IF THERE IS A PART of Paul's prescription for peace that
gets overlooked, it's this verse that tells us we need to be gentle
to all. Yet for many this is the pivotal verse, for it demands
evaluation and a change of attitude.

A businessman making an overnight car trip was forced to
pull over and stop when he had two flat tires. After replacing
one tire with the spare, he needed to take the other to an all-
night service station for repair.

Walking down the highway, he imagined an unpleasant
encounter: The repairman might be sleeping and could become
rude and unpleasant when awakened. The traveler rehearsed
his words, imagined the irate reaction of the repairman, and

planned his own response. The farther he walked, the more incensed he became. By the time he reached the station, he was so angry that he didn't wait for the repairman; he banged on the door and shouted, "Go ahead and sleep. I'll fix it myself!"

CONFLICT AND CONFRONTATION

Few of us have been in that traveler's situation, but the dialogue that took place in his mind may seem all too familiar. Too many of our walks down the highways of life are filled with thoughts of conflict and confrontation, either real or imaginary. We make assumptions about people's thinking, feelings, intentions, and reactions—probably based on what ours would be in similar situations. We disregard the words of Jesus, " 'Do not judge, or you too will be judged. For in the same way you judge others, you will be judged, and with the measure you use, it will be measured to you' " (Matthew 7:1–2).

We think we know the motives behind people's behavior, but do we? Jesus warned of the difficulty of making accurate evaluations in such situations: "How can you say to your brother, 'Let me take the speck out of your eye,' when all the time there is a plank in your own eye?" (Matthew 7:4).

What did Jesus mean when He spoke about judging others? Often it is thinking that we know the motives behind their actions and words. Paul warns us: "Judge nothing before the appointed time; wait till the Lord comes. He will bring to light what is hidden in darkness and will expose the motives of men's hearts" (1 Corinthians 4:5).

TOO TOUGH TO HANDLE

Our culture increasingly advocates an assertive "get in your face" philosophy: "Be rough, tough, and hard to bluff. Talk gruff. Don't take that stuff." We would be better off taking the following advice: "Don't fight. Don't take flight. Don't get uptight. Treat people right. Keep Jesus in sight."

Have you noticed that many of our anxieties have names and faces attached to them? We worry about people, and people worry about us. We disappoint people. They disappoint us. We fear the conflicts that might occur. We could reduce fear and gain inner tranquillity if we would determine to be gentle, kind, gracious, and considerate as the Bible says:

. . . .

> *"Love is patient, love is kind"* (1 CORINTHIANS 13:4).
> *"A gentle answer turns away wrath, but a harsh word stirs up anger"* (PROVERBS 15:1).
> *"Learn from me, for I am gentle and humble in heart"* (MATTHEW 11:29).

> *"Be kind and compassionate to one another,*
> *forgiving each other, just as in Christ God forgave*
> *you"* (EPHESIANS 4:32).
> *"Clothe yourselves with compassion, kindness,*
> *humility, gentleness and patience"* (COLOSSIANS 3:12).

Loren Cunningham, founder of Youth with a Mission, suggests that when we encounter people who have a poor attitude or even an evil spirit, we should approach them with the opposite attitude or spirit—choosing to be calm when others are angry, kind when others are mean, humble when others are proud, reasonable when others are belligerent…. The results can be startling!

FIRST-CLASS RESULTS OF KINDNESS

Dolly and I were waiting to board a flight from Minneapolis to Amsterdam. There had been a strike, and some of the passengers had been delayed for several days. The flight was overbooked. The atmosphere was tense.

We had bought our tickets at separate times, so we would not be seated together. Of course we wanted to change that, but the crowded scene offered us little hope.

We got to the gate and inserted our boarding cards into the ticket-taking device. Mine was accepted. Dolly's was not. We were told to step out of line and wait. The ticket agent looked at us and said to her colleague, "They're not going!"

As we waited, we considered three options: (1) be tough and demand our rights, (2) melt into the background and give up, (3) kindly communicate to the agent that we really needed to go and pray for a solution.

We chose the third option, sympathizing with her and treating her gently. Each time our eyes met, we smiled to let her know that we were hopeful but understanding.

When she finally handed us boarding cards, we asked if the seats were together. She said simply, "You'll like them."

We read the numbers, 73C and 73D, and headed for the back of the jumbo 747. When we got to the last seats in the plane and saw that the row number was 65, I asked the flight attendant, "Are we pulling a trailer today?" She laughed and said, "Go to the front of the plane."

So, dodging incoming passengers, we went to the front and were sent upstairs. We had been assigned first-class seats! (The "Hallelujah Chorus" plays here.)

Don't get me wrong. I'm not saying, "Be kind because that's the best technique to get what you want." I'm saying, "Be kind and understanding because God is kind, and He wants to show His kindness through us to others—whatever the outcome of our situation!"

IS MEEKNESS WEAKNESS?

God's words regarding gentleness are of particular importance to me because I'm a big guy, and sometimes I state my opinions forcefully. As a result, some people consider me intimidating—not the image I want to project, nor the way I want to be.

When I was a child, my favorite Bible character was Samson, the Spirit-empowered "tough guy." The Bible verse I least appreciated was, "If someone strikes you on one cheek, turn to him the other also" (Luke 6:29). While some liked the image of a gentle Jesus, meek and mild, I preferred the one of Jesus driving the money changers from the temple or calling the Pharisees "a brood of vipers" (see John 2:13–17 and Matthew 12:34).

I thought gentleness was a sign of fear—that "blessed are the meek" (Matthew 5:5) was for the weak. I now understand, as most of us do, that gentleness is a sign of strength, and the "tough guy" image is usually a cover for insecurity and the need to prove something to ourselves and to others. The fact that gentleness is essential to healthy relationships stands out in Paul's earnest plea to Christians: "Be completely humble and gentle; be patient, bearing with one another in love. Make every effort to keep the unity of the Spirit through the bond of peace" (Ephesians 4:2–3).

Although it couldn't be stated more clearly, many of us act tough and make only halfhearted attempts to improve relationships. Too often we leave the improvement up to others.

If only we could learn that when our *actions* are gentle, we have no reason to fear people's *reactions*. When we are kind, our conscience is clear, our mind is at rest, our heart is free, and we feel God's peace. But that may be easier said than done, as the saying goes!

CHRISTIANS...WITH ISSUES

How can we be kind to others if they are not kind to us? What if we simply can't find it in our heart to be kind?

An important verse of scripture recently spoke to me: "Above all else, guard your heart, for it is the wellspring of life" (Proverbs 4:23).

The King James Version says it this way: "Keep thy heart with all diligence; for out of it are the issues of life."

If we want to be at peace, we must guard our heart and its issues. God is telling us: Don't let your heart become bitter, hateful, or resentful. Don't let your heart remain deceitful or corrupt. Don't allow your heart to embrace impurity or lust. Don't permit your heart to become discouraged or cynical. Don't allow your heart to be divided in its purposes or desires. Don't give your heart any excuses to remain angry!

As Christians, the essential virtues of our faith are love and forgiveness. Our primary responsibility is to love God with our whole being and to love those around us as we love ourselves (see Matthew 22:37–40). Secondly, we are forgiven of our sins, failures, and offenses—*when we forgive others of theirs.*

We acknowledge these teachings, but do we follow them? Our angry conflicts and lack of inner peace are evidence that sometimes we do not love or forgive as we should. We hold grudges, nurture resentments, criticize others, despise their actions, avoid contact with them, and harden our hearts and allow them to throb with pain and anger when we think about what people have done to us. Believe me—I speak from experience!

MY OWN ISSUES

A few months before writing this book, I felt that I had been treated poorly. To me it was unacceptable, and whenever I thought or talked about it I relived the experience and felt anger and pain in my heart. If the issues had only affected me I think I could have let them go, but they also affected my friends, many of whom counted on my support.

I had previously written a book that stated: "We need to forgive completely, unconditionally, generously, verbally, volitionally, wholeheartedly, indiscriminately, and constantly."[1] Now I wondered if I could do it—or if I even wanted to!

I knew what biblical principles should be observed in situations like this, but I rationalized that they did not apply to my case. I thought that someone needed to speak up, and if no one else had the courage to do it, believe me, I did! I wanted the truth (as I saw it) told, people put in their place, and changes made. I wouldn't admit it—even to myself—but I thought that the people involved should experience a little of the discomfort my friends and I felt. I had always loved these people, but suddenly I found it hard to trust them.

Worse than the damaged friendships was the crisis in my walk with God. I continued to pray, read the Bible, witness to others, and serve the Lord, but the difficulty to do it increased and my joy diminished. Because I was not dealing with the issues in my heart, I could not get through to the heart of God, the heart of scripture, or the hearts of people.

"LET YOUR GENTLENESS
BE EVIDENT...."

Then I came across Paul's words in Philippians 4:5: "Let your gentleness be evident to all—the Lord is near." They were simple words, but I could not fulfill them. I had not guarded my heart, and even though I told myself to be gentle, my thoughts and words regarding the situation were bitter. I was trying to be kind when I was angry. I had written about forgiveness, but I was not forgiving. I was writing about peace, but I had none.

During a trip to the nation of Kosovo, I read the words of R. T. Kendall in his book *Total Forgiveness*: "The ultimate proof of total forgiveness is when we sincerely petition the Father to let off the hook those who have hurt us—even if they have hurt those close to us." He went on to say, "I will not hold people responsible for what they have done to me. I will hold nothing against them, and I will tell nobody what they have done."[2]

Kendall's words shined brightly into my darkness, and I saw that I needed to repent of my attitudes and forgive everyone involved—even though it would be difficult and I would do it more for my sake than for theirs.

I knew that none of the people had hurt me intentionally, so they probably didn't sense a need for my forgiveness. I was the one who had the need, and forgiving them met that need and freed me from my stress and discouragement. Now when I think of them, I don't have to restate my forgiveness for the four hundred and eighty-seventh time. My heart has filled with love for them.

THE LORD IS NEAR

Paul's instruction to be gentle in Philippians 4:5 is followed by four words—"The Lord is near." Why this connection?

I noticed that some versions refer at this point to Christ's Second Coming: "Let everyone see that you are gentle and kind. The Lord is coming soon" (NCV). That seemed right, because we all agree that when the Lord returns we will want to be known as kind, considerate persons.

But the more I studied the text, the more I thought "the Lord is near" could also refer to His closeness to us here and now. He sees all we do, hears all we say, and knows our thoughts. We must account for our actions and attitudes, both good and bad, before God. That's the sobering side of it. The encouraging side is that He is accessible when we want to be kind and need His help. We can call on Him at any time.

But there's yet another reason for Paul's reminding us that the Lord is near—it's so we will not grieve Him and lose the sense of His presence. "Do not grieve the Holy Spirit of God.... Be kind and compassionate" (Ephesians 4:30, 32).

Whatever Paul's reason for putting these phrases together, we can and must be gentle—because the Lord is near!

GIVE UP THE RIGHT TO BE RIGHT!

Too many times we insist on having the last word on an issue. We see ourselves as champions for truth, but it's often only our insistence to get our own way. When we've won the argument, what's the prize? To be seen as smarter, stronger, and more self-assured than others? Is it worth it?

Brazilian statesman Rui Barbosa once said, "He who does not fight for his rights is not worthy of them." Barbosa's words may be appropriate in a nation's struggle for freedom or justice for all races, genders, and classes of people. But when we're fighting for self-promotion, fulfillment, supremacy, the superiority of our ideas, or just to get what we want—we're engaged in a battle in which there is no winner.

God's Word lays it out clearly: "The Lord's servant must not quarrel; instead, he must be kind to everyone, able to teach, not resentful" (2 Timothy 2:24).

It is better to yield our "rights" to the Lord and allow Him to defend them. When we say that Jesus is Lord of our life, all the rights we previously claimed now belong to Him—including the right to be right. His example of yielding His rights tells us that we should also yield ours:

> *"Your attitude should be the same as that of Christ Jesus:*
> *who, being in very nature God, did not consider equality with*
> *God something to be grasped, but made himself nothing, taking*
> *the very nature of a servant, being made in human likeness.*
> *And being found in appearance as a man, he humbled himself*
> *and became obedient to death—even death on a cross!"*
> (PHILIPPIANS 2:5–8).

Are we gentle, or do we bully our way through life, defending ourselves and asserting our authority? We claim to love God and others, but how does our love compare to God's view of love? Here's what the Bible says about it in 1 Corinthians 13:4–5:

> *"Love is patient, love is kind. It does not envy, it does*
> *ot boast, it is not proud. It is not rude, it is not self-seeking,*
> *it is not easily angered, it keeps no record of wrongs."*

When I was in the midst of my struggle, I spent several nights awake, rehearsing in my mind what I wanted to say to the people with whom I disagreed. I was like the traveler in the beginning of the chapter. *"He'll say... I'll say..."* became the thoughts I went to bed with. Eventually I had the same conversations with the people involved.

Dolly lived through this time with me and had many of the same opinions I did, but she was more gracious than I was. One day, when I was working on this chapter, I read part of it to Dolly. As she listened, tears came to her eyes. She looked at me sadly and said, "Do you see that you are writing this for yourself?"

I did see it, and I asked myself, "Could Paul's little statement about kindness be even more important than I thought it was? Am I faithful to the Word and the Spirit of Christ in regard to this? Do I need to take my own words to heed?"

That's exactly what I needed to do! I still need to. Every day! All of us do.

Now let me ask you: Could this chapter also be for you? Are you as gentle with others as you should be? Are you in the midst of a struggle that makes it hard to be kind? Are you willing to join me in asking for the Holy Spirit's help?

As I already said: Don't fight. Don't take flight. Don't get uptight. Treat people right. Keep Jesus in sight.

For your own sake, for the sake of others, and to avoid grieving the Holy Spirit—make up your mind to be kind and call on Him when you need His help. Maybe that's what you need to do to discover a new peace of heart and mind.

"DO NOT BE ANXIOUS ABOUT ANYTHING."

PHILIPPIANS 4:6

DON'T SWEAT.
DON'T FRET.
DON'T GET UPSET.

SWEAT—THERE WAS A TIME when this word was not used in "polite company." *Perspiration* was a more acceptable word. Today we say "sweat" with a wide range of meanings. A noteworthy example is Richard Carlson's best seller *Don't Sweat the Small Stuff...and It's All Small Stuff.* "Sweat" now means anxiety, concern, worry, or preoccupation. No antiperspirant prevents it, disguises it, covers it, or removes it.

We don't like to admit it, but most of us worry more than we should. Some are natural worriers, seemingly born with a furrowed brow. Others learn the art as children or at puberty, marriage, parenthood, when their children reach puberty or start dating or whenever…. We may not know when we start or stop worrying—or if we ever do.

WHAT DO WE WORRY ABOUT?

There are countless causes for worry. Some of them come to us by design. For instance, insurance companies exploit our worries to sell policies. They send messages like: "If you got sick or were injured and couldn't work, what would happen to you and your family? Could you pay your bills when your expenses were increased and your ability to earn a living was reduced or eliminated?" Insurance is a wise investment, but the text insinuates that our worries will be eliminated if we buy their policy. Will they?

We worry about money, our kids, our health, our future, and perhaps some things that we cannot articulate:

What if…

—SOMETHING BRINGS HARM TO ME OR TO A FAMILY MEMBER?

—THE ECONOMY DOES NOT REBOUND, AS I NEED IT TO?

—MY INVESTMENTS FAIL TO BRING THE RETURN I NEED?

—I LOSE MY JOB?

—MY KIDS DO SOMETHING TO JEOPARDIZE THEIR FUTURE?

—MY HEALTH FAILS ME?

—I CAN NO LONGER TAKE CARE OF MYSELF?

—SOMEONE DISCOVERS WHAT I'M REALLY LIKE AND REJECTS ME?

—SOMEONE DISCOVERS THE SHAMEFUL THING I HAVE DONE?

—I EMBARRASS MYSELF?

WHY WORRY ABOUT WORRY?

The Random House Dictionary defines worry as "to torment oneself with disturbing thoughts." Worry is thinking in ways that bring uncertainty, insecurity, and discomfort. It's more than preparing for possible trouble; it's often irrational fear of trouble that may never come or might not be as bad as we imagine. Worry can affect us to the point that we're upset about everything while preparing for nothing.

Why does Paul write about worry? For several reasons— it's so common to us; it's not good for us; it accomplishes so little; and it dishonors the God who cares for us. Worry may be our most enduring form of unbelief.

Whatever you call it—worry, anxiety, or just "sweating it out"—Jesus and Paul agree: Don't do it! Jesus taught us not to worry about food, drink, clothes, tomorrow, the length of our lives, or what to say (Matthew 6:25–34). Paul used fewer but more inclusive words: Don't worry about anything!

GOD PROVIDES

God's message is not just "Don't worry." The message is, "You don't have to worry!" Our Father knows our needs and cares about meeting them. If we seek Him, obey Him, trust Him, and put Him first, things will come to us as we need them.

Dolly and I learned about this when we were young church-planters. Our earnings were low, our savings were nil, and we were committed to never going in debt or telling people about our needs. We would trust God alone.

It worked fine until one Sunday when we were out of money, out of food, and had just enough gas in our car to go to church and back. Sure that someone would invite us to lunch, we stood at the curb after the service until everyone drove away, leaving us no option but to drive home (coasting down every hill to save gas).

We walked into our apartment, sat down, and prepared to fast and pray—not by choice, not for pleasure, and not for any good reason. Within a few minutes the phone rang and a friend was on the line: "I don't know why we didn't think of it sooner, but we would like you to come for lunch."

Wonderful!—except for one thing: They lived on the opposite side of the city and we didn't have enough gas to get there and back.

When I started to say "We can't make it," my friend interrupted: "God told me to meet you at a gas station near your house, fill your tank, and invite you to lunch."

A lesson like that should last a lifetime, yet we found it easy to thank God for that provision and still doubt later that we would receive another one. Fortunately, God has been kind enough to repeat the lesson many times, along with another important one: We will not quit worrying unless we replace worry with better things.

Let me suggest a few.

REPLACE WORRY WITH HIGHER PRIORITIES

In speaking about worry, Jesus did not suggest indifference, denial, or mere positive thinking. In Matthew 6:31–33, He said the following:

> *"So do not worry, saying, 'What shall we eat?' or 'What shall we drink?' or 'What shall we wear?' For the pagans run after all these things, and your heavenly Father knows that you need them. But seek first his kingdom and his righteousness, and all these things will be given to you as well."*

The key, according to Jesus, is to put God first and trust Him to take care of us. Somehow we tend to turn things around. We get so concerned about ourselves, our wants, our needs, and our lives that we forget to put Him first.

Notice the order of priorities in the prayer that Jesus taught us to pray (see Matthew 6:9–13). Look at the difference between the first three requests and the second three:

FIRST: Hallowed be your name.
        Your kingdom come.
        Your will be done.

THEN: Supply our daily bread [needs].
        Forgive our trespasses.
        Free us from temptation and evil.

The first three requests concern God's purposes and require our action. We are to make holy or *hallow* His name, extend His kingdom, and do His will. The second three requests concern our needs and require God's action. His purposes, then our needs: That's the order God wants to see in our lives.

Many of our worries persist because we do not care for His interests as we should, so we wonder if we have the right to ask

Him to care for our needs. We forget that the Christian life is not about us; it's about Him! When we seek Him above other things, we don't find it hard to believe the encouraging words of Paul: "My God will meet all your needs according to his glorious riches in Christ Jesus" (Philippians 4:19).

REPLACE WORRY WITH INTEGRITY

Our lack of trust in God may cause us to take matters into our own hands and do questionable things that block what He wants to do for us. Then we may rationalize that our predicaments justify acts and words that are not completely honest or ethical. We hope He understands.

Of course He understands—better than we do—but does He approve? That's the first thing we worry about. The second is that our error will be exposed to others.

I once heard that politicians, from a nation I will not name, received a letter that stated, "The truth is out. We've been exposed." Within days, several of them left the country.

Paul wrote to his younger disciple Timothy: "The goal of this command is love, which comes from a pure heart and a good conscience and a sincere faith" (1 Timothy 1:5). He put this in

"First," said the doctor, "decide if starting on time is so important. Then lighten up. In this culture, it's unlikely that your people are going to be punctual."

The missionary was not satisfied. "I can't lighten up. What other options do you suggest?"

The doctor spelled it out: "There are no other options. You either lighten up, or you let it drive you crazy."

Think about your worries. Are they really so important? Are you making mountains of molehills? Richard Carlson is right: "Don't sweat the small stuff!" Keep it in perspective.

REPLACE WORRY WITH HOPE

The word *hope*, as used in the Bible, is much stronger than the expression "I hope so." It's more than a simple wish that things will turn out for the best.

Hope is the foundation upon which we build a positive frame of mind: It's confidence, assurance, optimism, and expectation— all with a focus on God! To hope is to trust in God and in His promises and character. To hope in God is to see Him as the source of all we need and trust that He will meet our need. Hope gives us the resilience to truly believe in a better tomorrow. God makes wonderful promises to those who hope in Him. "No one whose hope is in you will ever be put to shame" (Psalm 25:3).

When I studied Portuguese, I learned the versatile verb *esperar*, a single word that is used in Portuguese and Spanish to express verbs like *hope, expect, anticipate, wait,* or *desire.*

One day I sat in a Brazilian hotel room thinking about the usefulness and inclusiveness of this word. As I wrote the English equivalents on a sheet of paper, I looked out the window and saw a gorgeous rainbow—God's symbol of hope and His promise to save humanity rather than destroy it.

A discouraged psalmist once asked himself:

"Why are you downcast, O my soul? Why so disturbed within me?"

Then he preached himself a little sermon:

"Put your hope in God, for I will yet praise him, my Savior and my God" (PSALM 42:5–6).

As Christians we have the ultimate hope: Christ, the assurance of heaven. We don't say, as some do, "I hope to make it to heaven." We say, "My hope is built on nothing less than Jesus' blood and righteousness.... On Christ the solid Rock I stand. All other ground is sinking sand."[1]

REPLACE WORRY WITH TRUST

Jesus told His disciples, " 'Do not let your hearts be troubled. Trust in God; trust also in me' " (John 14:1).

We *believe* in Him, but do we really *trust* Him?

Shortly after the September 11, 2001, attacks on the World Trade Center and the Pentagon, an Internet survey asked Americans if they felt that their security was threatened. As a Midwesterner, I felt less threatened than people on the East Coast. But more important than my distance from the horrific scenes was my trust in God that the final chapters of history will not be written by terrorists, but by God Himself. Yes, we must do our part as individuals and as a nation, but ultimately we must rely upon God.

We must trust and not be afraid! When we don't understand what's happening around us or why it's happening, we must trust in God. We don't know the future, but we know Jesus— the Alpha and Omega, the Beginning and the End, the Author and Finisher of our faith!

A classic hymn helps us speak to our soul as the psalm writer did. We can draw strength from these words of Katherine von Schlegel, written more than two hundred years ago:

Be still my soul: thy God doth undertake
To guide the future, as He has the past.
Thy hope, thy confidence let nothing shake;
All now mysterious shall be bright at last.[2]

REPLACE WORRY WITH AN AWARENESS OF JESUS

Luke 24:13–35 tells us that after His resurrection, Jesus appeared to two of His followers as they walked the seven miles from Jerusalem to Emmaus. Here's the biblical text:

"Now that same day two of them were going to a village called Emmaus, about seven miles from Jerusalem. They were talking with each other about everything that had happened. As they talked and discussed these things with each other, Jesus himself came up and walked along with them; but they were kept from recognizing him.

He asked them, 'What are you discussing together as you walk along?'

They stood still, their faces downcast. One of them, named Cleopas, asked him, 'Are you only a visitor to Jerusalem and do not know the things that have happened there in these days?'

'What things?' he asked.

'About Jesus of Nazareth,' they replied. 'He was a prophet, powerful in word and deed before God and all the people. The chief priests and our rulers handed him over to be sentenced to death, and they crucified him; but we had hoped that he was the one who was going to redeem Israel. And what is more, it is the third day since all this took place. In addition, some of our women amazed us. They went to the tomb early this morning but didn't find his body. They came and told us that they had seen a vision of angels, who said he was alive. Then some of our companions went to the tomb and found it just as the women had said, but him they did not see.'

He said to them, 'How foolish you are, and how slow of heart to believe all that the prophets have spoken! Did not the Christ have to suffer these things and then enter his glory?' And beginning with Moses and all the Prophets, he explained to them what was said in all the Scriptures concerning himself.

As they approached the village to which they were going, Jesus acted as if he were going farther. But they urged him strongly, 'Stay with us, for it is nearly evening; the day is almost over.' So he went in to stay with them.

When he was at the table with them, he took bread, gave thanks, broke it and began to give it to them. Then their eyes

were opened and they recognized him, and he disappeared from
their sight. They asked each other, 'Were not our hearts burning
within us while he talked with us on the road and opened the
Scriptures to us?'

They got up and returned at once to Jerusalem. There they
found the Eleven and those with them, assembled together
and saying, 'It is true! The Lord has risen and has appeared to
Simon.' Then the two told what had happened on the way, and
how Jesus was recognized by them when he broke the bread."

The followers' disappointment in Christ's crucifixion shook them to the core and appeared to put all their hopes and dreams in jeopardy. Their words, body language, and tone of voice must have revealed total despondency. They probably said things like: "If He could heal the sick, drive out demons, raise the dead, walk on water, calm the seas, and inspire the multitudes, why couldn't He avoid such a shameful and humiliating death? Were we wrong? What good did it do to follow Him?"

They knew Jesus and loved Him, yet when Jesus fell in step with them and walked beside them, they didn't recognize Him. Was He disguising Himself so they could speak as common men and say what was on their hearts? Or was it their despondency that kept them from seeing who He was?

There are wonderful lessons to be found in Luke 24:13–35. Here are just a few of them:

JESUS COMES TO US IN OUR DEEPEST DISAPPOINTMENTS THROUGH WAYS WE DON'T ALWAYS RECOGNIZE. He walks with us when our hope is gone. He draws near when we feel far from Him. He does things for us that we can't see. He works in ways we don't understand. Are we aware of His presence?

JESUS ENCOURAGES US TO SHARE OUR HEARTACHES, AND HE LISTENS AS WE POUR OUT OUR HEARTS TO HIM. What concerns do we need to share with Jesus today? What keeps us from sharing our troubles with Him? A sense of unworthiness, shame, or despair? What cares can we share only with Him? What persons around us need someone to listen to them?

JESUS TAKES OUR CONFUSION TO GOD'S WORD. He wants to make His Word real to us, but sometimes we neglect the Bible when we need it most. Are we reading it? Are we drawing strength from it? What might Jesus want to say to us from His Word?

JESUS ACCEPTS OUR INVITATION TO BECOME MORE DEEPLY INVOLVED IN OUR LIVES. It appeared that Jesus would continue on His way, but He had walked with them to the place where they must either let Him go or invite Him to stay. We don't need to beg, but we must ask. In what specific areas of our lives do we need to ask for Jesus' further involvement?

JESUS REVEALS HIMSELF TO US IN FAMILIAR PATTERNS. They had seen it many times: He took bread, blessed it, broke it, and gave it. Our times of trouble, stress, and anxiety are not times to abandon the routines that bring us strength or the people who bring us encouragement. We must remember that things change, policies change, and people change, but God does not change—and He is with us as He has always been!

JESUS RESTORES OUR HOPE AND OUR PASSION AND GIVES US A MESSAGE OF LIFE TO SHARE WITH OTHERS. Even when we have lost hope, it can be restored and our passion renewed. What needs to be restored in our lives today?

Faith? Courage? Vision? Hope? Excitement? Purpose? The
disciples, despite the long walk they had just taken, became
energized and returned to Jerusalem to share their good news.
What message must we proclaim?

REPLACE WORRY WITH ACTION

The problem with worrying about tomorrow is that it takes
our focus off of what we need to do today. We need to *prepare*
for tomorrow rather than *worry* about it.

Are you worried about your health? Get a checkup.

Worried about your job? Ask for a review.

Worried about investments? Get some advice.

Worried about your kids? Talk to them.

What we must *not* do is procrastinate or retreat to a comfort
zone like television, food, inactivity, or chemical dependence.
Our comfort zones fail us because they only offer distraction.
We need action more than distraction. We need the reassurance
that only comes by doing something!

I have a sign in my office that says, "Don't delay! It doesn't
pay. It won't go away! Do it today!" It tells me that, whatever
I do, I need to do it decisively. Procrastination increases
stress. I need to act—even if my action is to ask God
to act for me.

God often conditions His promises of blessing to His calls for action. There is hope in verses like these:

> *"Cast your cares on the LORD and he will sustain you"*
> (PSALM 55:22).
> *"Commit to the LORD whatever you do, and your plans will succeed"* (PROVERBS 16:3).
> *"Cast all your anxiety on him because he cares for you"*
> (1 PETER 5:7).

Cast! Commit! Confide! When things are out of control, we must learn to commit them to the Lord and trust Him to achieve His purpose and see us through our troubles. We'll never defeat our fears by fleeing from them. We'll defeat them by facing them head-on while trusting completely in God.

REPLACE WORRY WITH GOALS

We all need a good reason for getting up in the morning. We need more than something to do; we need something to accomplish! Is there anything more tiring than working without a sense of direction and accomplishment? It's the vision of accomplishment that provides the motivation and the energy to work hard. Scripture advises: "Whatever your hand finds to do, do it with all your might, for in the grave, where you are going, there is neither working nor planning nor knowledge nor wisdom" (Ecclesiastes 9:10).

Working, planning, acquiring knowledge, and applying wisdom are great ways to avoid worry and stress. Each of these activities can then be broken down into short, measurable goals. We need to do more than take steps; we need to know where the steps are taking us. Otherwise, we lose heart.

I was impressed the other day by the simplicity and clarity of a prayer offered by Dr. Sudhir Isaiah, a distinguished Christian leader visiting from Singapore: "Lord, help us not to just do Your work; help us to do Your will."

How about setting some God-given goals to honor Him, to get His direction, and to relieve your stress?

REPLACE WORRY WITH GOD'S WORD

What better way to rid yourself of your worry-filled point of view than to replace it with God's point of view? The Bible is Spirit-breathed and different from any other book. It's filled with wise counsel and with life! It's our great weapon to overcome temptation. Each time Jesus was tempted by Satan, He answered with the words, "It is written...."

In his book *The Purpose-Driven Life*, Rick Warren writes, "The Bible is far more than a doctrinal guidebook. God's Word generates life, creates faith, produces change, frightens the devil, causes miracles, heals hurts, builds character, transforms circumstances, imparts joy, overcomes adversity, defeats temptation, infuses hope, releases power, cleanses our minds, brings things into being, and guarantees our future forever! We cannot live without the Word of God! Never take it for granted. You should consider it as essential to your life as food."[3]

ONE LAST THING...

I've suggested several alternatives to worry. However, I've intentionally left out the most important one because it deserves a chapter of its own: When the Bible tells us to worry about nothing, it also says to pray about everything.

Let's see what that's about!

"IN EVERYTHING, BY PRAYER AND PETITION..."

PHILIPPIANS 4:6

MAKE A WAY TO PRAY EVERY DAY

THE OLD GOSPEL SONG says it all:

> *O what peace we often forfeit,*
> *O what needless pain we bear,*
> *All because we do not carry*
> *Everything to God in prayer.*[1]

Christians have known for centuries what modern studies confirm: People who make prayer a significant part of their daily schedule tend to live longer, healthier, happier, more peaceful, and more productive lives. In prayer we gain deeper intimacy with God, peace, hope, courage, strength, and solutions to our problems. When we place our challenges and concerns in God's hands, we can face them confidently, knowing that He is always working on our behalf.

If this is true, we have to admit that when we don't feel peace of heart and mind…when we don't find hope, courage, and strength…when we fail to obtain solutions to our problems… it may be because we have neglected the time with God that would have brought all of these things to us.

Sometimes, rather than going to the Source of all we need, we seek comfort in food, entertainment, excessive activity, or inactivity that bring only temporary relief and no lasting value. We neglect the Bible. We neglect prayer. We neglect God— precisely at the time we need Him the most.

Andrew Murray makes an intriguing statement in his book *Teach Us to Pray*: "Though in its beginnings prayer is so simple that even a small child can pray, it is at the same time the highest and holiest work to which anyone can rise."[2]

I've observed that the move from a child's prayer to a mature prayer is not always easy and is many times poorly made. Instead of rising up to pray dynamic, confident prayers, we shrink into a passive mode and pray weak, ambiguous prayers. We may pray "God's will be done" when, in reality, we mean "Whatever…." Sometimes instead of gaining the understanding that makes prayer a powerful, positive experience, we make it much more complicated, difficult, and discouraging than it needs to be.

When we feel ambivalent about prayer, we are not alone. Most of us have had prayer times that brought us a sense of God's nearness and the confidence that we would receive an answer to our requests—but we've also had times when God seemed distant and we've wondered if our prayers did any good at all. A few years ago I put some of those feelings into a verse that perhaps expresses what many people feel today.

DO YOU HEAR MY PRAYER?

Are you listening to me, God?
Do You hear me when I pray?
Do You pay attention to what
I feel and do and say?

Am I sincere before You?
Do I pray with all my heart?
Or do I just say empty words?
Just act out a part?

You respond to deep desires,
Prayed with faith in Jesus' name,
When my will and Yours
Become the same.

But when I've been indifferent,
When I've neglected prayer—
Can I find my way to You?
Will You be there?

And if I've lost my focus?
If other things have filled my life?
If sin has found a home in me
And brought me pain and strife?

Without You, God, I'm helpless.
I'm weak and You are strong.
I need You when I'm right.
I need You when I'm wrong.

My Savior stands before You.
His wounds appear before Your face.

He offered You His precious blood.
He offers me His grace.

And so I know You hear me.
You accept me in my Savior's name.
It's not just because I've come.
It's because Jesus came.

Pour out your heart, You say.
Cast on Me your every care.
Everything that's too heavy
For you to bear.

I come to You today repentant.
Because I know You're there.
What strength and peace and power
I find in prayer.[3]

Maybe the disciples were facing some of the issues addressed
in this poem when they saw the connection between the prayers
of Jesus and the miracles that resulted from them. The difference
between His power-filled prayers and their powerless prayers
made them desperate enough to plead, "Lord, teach us to pray,

as John also taught his disciples" (Luke 11:1 NKJV).

What did Jesus teach them?

PRAY FOUNDATIONAL PRAYERS

In response to the disciples' request, Jesus taught them three lessons on prayer.

His first teaching (Luke 11:2–4) is a structure to guide us as we formulate the prayers we offer to God. We know it well:

> *"Our Father in heaven, hallowed be your name. Your kingdom come. Your will be done on earth as it is in heaven. Give us day by day our daily bread. And forgive us our sins, for we also forgive everyone who is indebted to us. And do not lead us into temptation, but deliver us from the evil one"* (NKJV).

This is a concise yet complete foundation on which we can build our prayers to God, expanding as we go, as illustrated here:

—MAY YOUR KINGDOM COME TO MY HEART, MY FAMILY, AND MY
BUSINESS. I WANT YOU TO OCCUPY AND GUIDE EVERY AREA
OF MY LIFE, MY FAMILY, MY CHURCH, MY CITY, MY NATION....
—FORGIVE MY SIN OF PRAYERLESSNESS, MY INDIFFERENCE
TO THE NEEDS OF OTHERS, MY LACK OF COURAGE TO STAND

By letting the Lord's model prayer remind us of the issues that surround us, we can construct a prayer life that will deal with His concerns and ours. By entrusting the basic issues of our lives to God, we gain peace of heart and mind.

PRAY BOLD, PERSISTENT PRAYERS

The Lord's second teaching on prayer (Luke 11:5–10) is about boldness and perseverance:

"Suppose one of you has a friend, and he goes to him at midnight and says, 'Friend, lend me three loaves of bread, because a friend of mine on a journey has come to me, and I have nothing to set before him.'

Then the one inside answers, 'Don't bother me. The door is already locked, and my children are with me in bed. I can't get up and give you anything.'

I tell you, though he will not get up and give him the bread because he is his friend, yet because of the man's boldness he will get up and give him as much as he needs.

So I say to you: Ask and it will be given to you; seek and you will find; knock and the door will be opened to you. For everyone who asks receives; he who seeks finds; and to him who knocks, the door will be opened."

Although the man discovers that his neighbor does not want to be inconvenienced, he persists until the neighbor's desire to get rid of him is greater than his desire to stay in bed. Jesus wants us to be bold and persistent with God.

When my friend Larry was a boy, his family raised chickens in a yard that was enclosed by a slatted snow fence. He says that sometimes a slat or two would break, and a chicken would escape.

At feeding time, the chicken would try to get back in but could not find the break in the fence. It would walk nearly the full length of the yard, inserting its head between each pair of slats to see if there was space enough for its body to follow.

Often when it nearly reached the opening, it would stop and go back the other way, repeating the process without success. It would come so close and yet remain outside.

Why does that happen in prayer? I'm convinced that God hears us each time we pray and is preparing an answer. Because, however, the answer sometimes depends on the cooperation of other people or a sequence of events that must take place, it takes longer than we think it should. We are close to a breakthrough when we lose faith and give up with the answer so close to us. A delay is not a denial. We must ask until we receive, seek until we find, and knock until the door opens.

PRAY INTIMATE PRAYERS

The third teaching of Jesus about prayer (Luke 11:11–13) reveals that God answers us because He is a gracious Father who loves us and desires the best for us.

> *"Which of you fathers, if your son asks for a fish, will give him a snake instead? Or if he asks for an egg, will give him a scorpion? If you then, though you are evil, know how to give good gifts to your children, how much more will your Father in heaven give the Holy Spirit to those who ask him!"*

What a privilege is ours! We can take our concerns and issues not just to a neighbor, lawyer, doctor, consultant, friend, or even an earthly father with limited skill and interest—we take them to the One who is an expert in every field, who also happens to be our loving heavenly Father.

I've heard it said that God always answers prayer; His answers are either "Yes," "No," or "Wait a while." I prefer to think that

His answers are either "Yes, I'll do it now"; "Yes, I'm working on it"; "Yes, but I have something better in mind."

God so loves to answer prayer that He seeks prayers to answer! They are opportunities to show His power and faithfulness to those who hunger for Him and to those who are willing to give Him the honor and the praise when He answers.

In these three teachings we have (1) a foundation upon which we can build our prayers, (2) a call to pray boldly and persistently, and (3) the assurance that our loving heavenly Father takes pleasure in answering our prayers.

A WIDE RANGE OF TOPICS FOR PRAYER

The Bible teaches us to pray alone and in groups; to pray for loved ones and for enemies; to pray with contrition and with a clear conscience, with faith and with fervor, with patience and with persistence—all with the guidance and empowering of the Holy Spirit. We should pray for nations and national leaders; for Christian workers and family members; for salvation for the lost, healing for the sick, and deliverance for the oppressed. Pushing it a bit further, Paul says, "In *everything*, by prayer and petition...present your requests to God" (Philippians 4:6, italics added).

I've thought about that word *everything*. What does it mean? I suspect that the use of this word is better understood by reading the entire passage than by isolating the verse. Remember, this text is about finding peace of heart and mind. That being true, we should pray about issues that trouble us, situations that worry us, people who perplex us, and problems that distress us. If it's important enough to think about, plan about, and worry about—it's important enough to pray about. It comes down to this: Never worry! Always pray!

God wants to draw us into a closer relationship where we collaborate with Him to achieve His purposes for His glory and our good. He wants to teach us to pray and to never give up. He wants us to pray with all our heart and to know that, when we do, we will find Him and His solutions to our problems:

"I know the plans I have for you…plans to prosper you and not to harm you, plans to give you hope and a future. Then you will call upon me and come and pray to me, and I will listen to you. You will seek me and find me when you seek me with all your heart" (JEREMIAH 29:11–13).

Consider the words "with all your heart." God is saying…

PRAY FERVENT PRAYERS

Israel's king David was a busy man—but a man who found time to be alone with God and pray fervent prayers. If ever anyone valued time alone with God, David did. Before his coronation, he was pursued by Saul's warriors, who sought to kill him. Moving from cave to cave to escape death, David found strength in the Lord and composed a psalm in which he says: "Trust in him at all times, O people; pour out your hearts to him, for God is our refuge" (Psalm 62:8).

It's one thing to memorize prayers, read prayers, or even pray extemporaneous prayers in a cold, mechanical way. Prayer can become an almost meaningless ritual. It's quite different when we learn to pour out our hearts and turn our worries into the fervent, effectual prayers that avail much (see James 5:16 KJV).

Obligations, entertainment, and comfort options lull us into passivity regarding prayer. We become the "lukewarm" Christians who, according to the Bible, are repulsive to God (see Revelation 3:16). Isaiah complained to God about such people: "No one calls on your name or strives to lay hold of you" (Isaiah 64:7).

When we find ourselves in that condition, we must discover the hindrance to prayer, root it out of our lives, and take hold of the privilege we have of appearing before God. Whether it's because of an unforgiving heart, feelings of guilt, an excessive sense of unworthiness, or unconfessed sin—we must not allow passivity to rule us. We must concentrate in prayer until our passion is rekindled and we can pray with the strong desire Jesus described: "What things soever ye desire, when ye pray, believe that ye receive them, and ye shall have them" (Mark 11:24 KJV).

Real prayer is not just words; nor is it just desire. Prayer is our heart's desire put into words. Sometimes we pray one thing while we desire another. Which is really a prayer?

Consider the desire expressed by these men and women of the Bible, and allow God to stir your heart in a similar way:

When Nehemiah heard that Jerusalem was in ruins, he wept, prayed, and fasted until the Spirit moved him to mobilize God's people to work (Nehemiah 1).

When Mordecai uncovered a plan to destroy the Jews, he tore his clothes, wore sackcloth, and walked the streets weeping until God gave him a plan to save them (Esther 4).

When Hannah was desperate for a child, she wept, made a vow, and prayed until God gave her a promise and then a son (1 Samuel 1).

When Jesus prepared to select His disciples, He prayed all night and then chose twelve. When He went to Lazarus's tomb, He wept, prayed, and resurrected Lazarus. When He prayed in the Garden of Gethsemane, He sweat drops of blood and then faced the cross (Luke 4–5; John 11; Luke 22:44).

Intensity is more important than ability because the Holy Spirit helps us overcome our inability. "We do not know what we ought to pray for, but the Spirit himself intercedes for us with groans that words cannot express" (Romans 8:26). He also wants to help us with our passivity. When our prayers become earnest desires and our desires become earnest prayers, we get answers from God.

PRAY WRITTEN PRAYERS

Let me make a suggestion about prayer that doesn't come directly from the Bible but is in perfect harmony with it— and one I have found extremely useful: Pray written prayers.

I'm part of a group that meets to pray for missionaries around the world. We usually read a few verses of scripture followed by a printed list of prayer requests. Then we add last-minute spoken requests. After that, each of us prays out loud for one or more of the requests while the others join in support of the prayer.

Having a written request is like having a claim ticket for an item we send out for repairs. Isn't it true that many of our prayers are requests to God for repairs? We remind the Lord that the job needs to be done, and He reminds us that the problem is in His hands.

Written prayers were important to me when I was asked to lead a mission in Brazil. At the outset, I identified seven problems that needed to have solutions. I wrote the problems on paper and told God I needed answers. What a blessing it was to see Him solve each problem decisively!

God has given us written promises that put Him on record as saying that He will answer. Written prayers put us on record as saying that we have asked. It's as though a contract were written that is binding upon both parties. God doesn't need that contract, but perhaps we do. God has taken the trouble to write to us. Why not write to Him?

PRAY HONEST PRAYERS

Sometimes we're like the man who said to Jesus, "I do believe; help me overcome my unbelief!" (Mark 9:24). That's an honest prayer. Although unbelief is wrong—especially considering the gracious and powerful character of God—we know that God is ready to meet us where we are and lead us to greater faith—if we will look to Him.

We need to see God as holy, exalted, and transcendent—so we stand in awe of Him. We also must see Him as loving, accepting, and immanent—so we can be honest with Him.

When the disciples asked Jesus to teach them to pray, they admitted that they were not praying well. That admission is the best place to start. "We do not know how to pray" is a prayer that makes us dependent upon God's Spirit with only one direction to go—forward! God has no greater pleasure than seeing His followers develop a life of effective prayer.

PRAY PURPOSEFUL PRAYERS

Knowing my own needs in relation to my walk with God, I find myself repeating many of the same requests to Him. There are certain requests that make their way into my devotional time with increasing frequency:

Help me, Lord, to…

—MAKE MY HEART ENTIRELY YOURS.

—ENJOY AN INTIMATE WALK WITH YOU.

—EMBRACE WHAT PLEASES YOU AND AVOID WHAT GRIEVES YOU.

—INVEST MY LIFE IN THE GROWTH OF YOUR KINGDOM.

—WALK IN LOVE AND TRUTH WITH MY COLLEAGUES.

—TRUST YOU FULLY.

—BE GUIDED AND EMPOWERED BY THE HOLY SPIRIT.

—SERVE PEOPLE WITH COMPASSION AND DISCERNMENT.

These prayers help me to focus on the life I want to live and measure myself against the goals I set for my walk with God.

PRAY BIBLICAL PRAYERS

The way we learn to pray is by praying. To guide us, we have the Holy Spirit and the Bible—with its sure and certain words. The following verses provide guidance for our life of prayer:

1. PRAY ALONE TO THE FATHER. " 'When you pray, go into your room, close the door and pray to your Father' " (Matthew 6:6).

2. PRAY WITH HUMILITY. "God opposes the proud but gives grace to the humble" (1 Peter 5:5).

3. PRAY IN JESUS' NAME. Jesus said, " 'No one comes to the Father except through me' " (John 14:6). " 'I will do whatever you ask in my name' " (John 14:13).

4. PRAY WITH A CLEAR CONSCIENCE. Go to God and anyone you have wronged. Ask for forgiveness and make it right. "If I had known of any sin in my heart, the Lord would not have listened to me" (Psalm 66:18 NCV).

5. PRAY WITH A THANKFUL HEART AND THANKFUL WORDS. "Give thanks whatever happens. That is what God wants for you in Christ Jesus" (1 Thessalonians 5:18 NCV).

6. PRAY OFTEN. Early morning is a good time to enjoy God's presence. "Fill us with your love every morning. Then we will sing and rejoice all our lives" (Psalm 90:14 NCV).

7. PRAY WITH FAITH. " 'So I tell you to believe that you have received the things you ask for in prayer, and God will give them to you' " (Mark 11:24 NCV).

8. PRAY IN SIMPLE WORDS. Don't imitate other people. Use your own words—not "vain repetitions" (Matthew 6:7 KJV).

9. PRAY IN HARMONY WITH GOD'S WILL. "He hears us whenever we ask for anything that pleases him. And since we know he hears us when we make our requests, we also know that he will give us what we ask for" (1 John 5:14–15 NLT).

10. PRAY PERSISTENTLY. " 'Ask, and it will be given to you; seek, and you will find; knock, and it will be opened to you' " (Luke 11:9 NKJV).

11. PRAY WITH A PARTNER. " 'If two of you on earth agree about anything you ask for, it will be done for you by my Father in heaven. For where two or three come together in my name, there am I with them' " (Matthew 18:19–20).

Joseph Scriven's song "What a Friend We Have in Jesus" not only speaks of the peace we forfeit and the pain we bear, but it also reminds us: "What a privilege to carry everything to God in prayer."[4]

We can pray our way to peace of heart and mind.

"WITH THANKSGIVING..."

PHILIPPIANS 4:6

MAKE GRATITUDE
YOUR ATTITUDE

DRIVING HOME FROM A WEDDING one winter
night in Minnesota, I watched the weather carefully, as sensible
Minnesotans do. Gusting winds brought blasts of snow across
the highway, but driving conditions seemed reasonable.

I was following a pickup truck from what I thought was
a safe distance when, without warning, the pickup went into
a spin, hit the rail on the left, and deflected directly into
my path.

Purely by reflex, I veered to the right and braced for the
impending collision. Not more than a second or two went by
and, to my amazement, the truck was behind me. I had gone
safely by without a scratch!

Too overcome with emotion to understand or even look back, I shouted, *"Thank You, God!"* with such force that I was as surprised by my outburst as the incident itself. I drove the rest of the way home praising God for a miraculous escape. I knew that both vehicles and at least two lives had been kept from a serious accident.

Arriving home, I told Dolly what had happened, and she joined me in praising God for His protection. Later I thanked Him that His presence in my life had not only guarded me but also caused an automatic response of thanksgiving. I was thankful to be safe and thankful to be thankful!

"WITH THANKSGIVING"

The New International Version rendition of Paul's words in Philippians 4:6 is awkward: "In everything, by prayer and petition, *with thanksgiving,* present your requests to God" (italics added). It makes thanksgiving seem like a last-minute thought, which certainly is not the case. Awkward as it may be, *thanksgiving* in the midst of words like *prayer, petition,* and *requests* could never be out of place. To pray, petition, and request with a thankful heart indicates that as our prayers rise to heaven we believe they will be answered, and we are thankful for the answer before we receive it.

Thanksgiving is essential to the communication with God that we call prayer. Again and again the words *give thanks* or *thank God* are repeated in the Bible.

Paul told New Testament Christians that he prayed for them with thanksgiving:

> *"We always thank God, the Father of our Lord Jesus Christ, when we pray for you"* (COLOSSIANS 1:3).

Besides praying for Christians, Paul encouraged them to pray and give thanks for each other:

> *"I urge…that requests, prayers, intercession and thanksgiving be made for everyone"* (1 TIMOTHY 2:1).

The writer to the Hebrews called thanksgiving an acceptable way to worship God:

> *"Let us be thankful, and so worship God acceptably with reverence and awe"* (HEBREWS 12:28).

WHEN WE FAIL TO GIVE THANKS

Jesus was disappointed that, after He healed a group of ten lepers, only one returned to give thanks (Luke 17:12–19).

> *"Jesus asked, 'Were not all ten cleansed? Where are the other nine? Was no one found to return and give praise to God except this foreigner?' Then he said to him, 'Rise and go; your faith has made you well.' "*

What prevented the other nine lepers from thanking Jesus for their healing? There could be several reasons. Perhaps as Jewish citizens they felt entitlement rather than gratitude. Do we ever take God's blessings for granted? The foreigner didn't feel entitlement. He knew that he was fortunate to get in on a blessing that Jesus provided for the Jewish people. How does God see it when we fail to show Him genuine thankfulness?

Gratitude may be the healthiest of all attitudes we can show. Lack of it may be the most dangerous one. If you are like me, you react to complaining and ingratitude in a negative way. When I hear people talk about all their problems and recite a litany of everything that is wrong, I feel like saying, "Grow up! Deal with it! Look at the bright side! Quit complaining; it's so childish!"

When Paul described the process that led humanity away from a relationship with God, he cited two important factors:

"When they knew God, they glorified him not as God, neither were thankful" (ROMANS 1:21 KJV).

GRATITUDE AND FAITH

Thanksgiving is more than an expression of gratitude; it's a springboard to faith. It reminds us that God has always been with us, is with us now, and will always be with us. Nothing dispels discouragement faster than remembering what God has done for us—and thanking Him for it!

That was the case with the late Mark Buntain, a missionary who had many responsibilities and a wonderful ministry in Calcutta, India. Leader of a thriving church, an important medical clinic, a modern school, and compassionate ministries to needy people of many descriptions, Mark Buntain was a man of God in his divinely appointed place.

But sometimes a situation would overwhelm him. There were so many urgent needs and never enough resources to meet all of them. Often when Mark became discouraged, his colleagues would send a new employee to his office and have him ask, "Pastor Mark, please tell me how this work began."

The man of God would then tell the story, including many of the miracles God had done. Before long his heart would fill with thanksgiving to God, his spirits would lift, and his faith would surge.

WHEN GOD DOES SOMETHING SPECIAL

When our faith is tested, I can think of nothing more encouraging than to look back to things God has done in our lives, things that only God could do, things that are so obviously of God that no one can take them away from us.

I recently looked back on several of those uncontestable works of God in my life. I could never doubt that God provided for my salvation through Christ, for my education, or that He led me in the choice of a calling and a life's companion. A miraculous healing that came to Dolly at a crucial time in our lives was a tremendous encouragement when it occurred and still is as we remember it today.

But I want to share an experience that will always be a reference point in our lives. It took place at a time when we were being tested, and it reminded us that God was with us and is with us even when we don't feel His presence.

On a trip to Brazil a few years ago, we wanted to visit Sonia, a Brazilian missionary who had undergone surgery to remove several tumors. We were told that she was staying with family members in Niterói, the city that lies across Guanabara Bay from the larger city of Rio de Janeiro. We had the address and followed the instructions to the city and to the neighborhood. We started looking for the street and the house.

After searching for a few minutes, we asked a taxi driver for help. He had never heard of the street but offered to call his dispatcher, who—he assured us—knew every street in the city. He placed the call and then reported to us that his all-knowing dispatcher had never heard of the street.

Puzzled, we went to a public telephone to call the missionary's husband. As I stood in line to use the phone, I overheard the man who was using it say, "Yes, she had the surgery. They removed some tumors, but more have appeared. They say they will have to operate again." He was giving a perfect description of Sonia's condition.

My curiosity peaked when a young man stepped up, said something to the man on the phone, and stepped away. I asked him to locate the street for me.

When he saw the address, he looked at me with a strange expression and said, "You have the right city and the right neighborhood, but the street you have written here is across the bay in Rio de Janeiro. As a matter of fact, you have my address! Why do you want to go there?"

"We want to visit a friend named Sonia and pray with her."

"Sonia is my sister," he said. "What a coincidence!"

I answered, "I don't think it is a coincidence. I believe that God led us to you."

"Well," he said, "God did a good job. Sonia is not at my house now. You are standing in front of the apartment where Sonia is staying!"

He introduced me to the man who had been speaking on the phone: "This is Sonia's father."

The father, too, was amazed and took us to the apartment, where we found Sonia and her whole family. They were all impressed that God had led us in such an extraordinary way and felt that something special was about to happen. When we joined in prayer for Sonia, the tumors were instantly and miraculously healed. She did not have the second operation and has been tumor-free for several years!

Every time I think about that experience I feel encouraged in my faith. How could I doubt that God was with us then or that He is with us now? How could I fail to thank Him?

But I do fail. Sometimes I let adverse circumstances block out my memories of God's provision. Unfortunately, I have not completely forgotten the well-developed art of doubting and complaining. I need to remember to thank God always, such as...

WHEN THINGS GO WRONG

Starting a printing and publishing ministry in Brazil was not an easy task. As young, inexperienced missionaries, we were grateful that generous contributions paid for a building and equipment and provided some of our support. Still, it took hard work and sacrifice to build a business and a ministry. We made lots of mistakes and often didn't know what to do.

Several missionary families lived and worked in crowded quarters and shared three vehicles for business, ministry, and personal use. At a staff meeting, we discussed our need for another vehicle and our lack of funds to buy one. After prayer, we decided to take up the subject at a later date.

That Saturday, two of the cars were in the shop for repairs, and I needed the third one to fulfill a commitment to a ministry on the opposite side of the city. Chuck Easterday, our leader, approached me. "I have to pick up an American couple at the bus station at four o'clock. Can you be back in time?"

"Sure, Chuck, no problem." I was glad for a reason to get back early.

The visit to the ministry went well, but when it was almost time to return, a missionary appeared at the door.

"I have two flat tires," he explained. "I'll have to get one of them to town to fix it. Can you take me?"

With no other solution in sight for him, I drove him to a repair shop in the little town of Betim.

As I handed the tire to the repairman I noticed that it had almost no tread remaining. I wondered what the inner tube was like. Urging him to work quickly, I watched as he applied a patch to the tube and placed it in a tub of water to test for leaks. The rising bubbles revealed that there was more work to be done. By the time he finished, there were four new patches on the tube, applied one at a time, with too much time spent on each one.

I drove back to the center; dropped off the missionary and his tire; picked up Terry McDowell, a young friend who had accompanied me; and headed directly for the bus station. There would be no time to get the car to Chuck.

The road was clear, and we covered ground on the gravel road like a Brazilian racing team until we approached the asphalt highway that would take us downtown. About one hundred feet from the highway we saw two huge freight trains stopped on the tracks with no sign of movement and no way around them!

As we waited for the trains to move, every minute seemed like ten. I tapped nervously on the steering wheel until Terry faced me and said, "George, I think we need to praise God!"

"Praise God?" I asked "Why do you say that, Terry?"

"I've been reading a book called *Prison to Praise* by Merlin Carothers, which says we should give thanks to God in every circumstance we face."

I had read the book and knew it was based on Paul's challenge: "Give thanks in all circumstances, for this is God's will for you in Christ Jesus" (1 Thessalonians 5:18). Truthfully, I wasn't in the mood to offer praises, but since the command is so clear, I couldn't disagree. It took some effort, but when words of praise and thanksgiving left my lips, I felt more relaxed and thought of the well-known scripture verse "All things work together for good to those who love God, to those who are the called according to His purpose" (Romans 8:28 NKJV).

I sensed that God was working and the situation would turn out for the best. Within a few minutes, the trains left and we headed for the bus station, hoping that Chuck would meet us there.

When we arrived at the station, the American visitors were standing at a counter enjoying ice cream. We introduced ourselves, apologized for the delay, and explained that it only happened because our mission needed another car.

When Chuck showed up, after taking the bus to the station, he explained the situation again. The visitors were gracious as we loaded up and took them home.

The next day I needed the car again, but so did Chuck. My appointment was farther away and could not be postponed. Chuck approached me: "Our guests have invited Karen and me to lunch. Can you help us?"

We agreed that I would drop the two couples at a restaurant where they would eat and then catch a taxi home. It would be inconvenient, but it would work.

Later, Chuck told me what took place. As they finished eating, the American said, "Our church likes to send funds to missionary projects. Do you have one for us?"

Not knowing what kind of project the church could afford, Chuck was hesitant. "We always have needs," he replied.

The visitor said, "It seems to me that you need a car!"

Chuck answered, "Yes, we do."

"We're going to buy it for you!" the visitor announced.

And they did—a beautiful new station wagon, the first new car our mission had ever owned!

Would the church have provided the car if we had not given praise to God? Possibly. Would they have purchased it if our troubles had not pointed out the need? Only God knows the answer to that question. What we did know was that we were suddenly thankful for the inconveniences we had experienced.

We may face difficult circumstances and wonder why things go wrong. We may have to go on with no explanation from God, but we should not assume that things are out of control. Things may be out of *our* control, but they are never outside of God's. His love is pure, His word is secure, His help is sure, so we can endure. Let us always be thankful and praise Him by faith even before the solution comes.

WHEN LOSS BECOMES GAIN

Let me tell you about Nathan and Ali. Nathan is from Southern California, where he grew up in a pastor's home. Ali came from the north coast of Wales, the daughter of a physician. Nathan and Ali were both led by God to study at Bethany College of Missions in Minneapolis.

At Bethany they met, married, and prepared to serve in Central or Eastern Europe. Ali had done previous work in Romania, but I suggested to them Slovenia, where our mission has church-planting teams and where I thought they would fit well. They decided to have a look.

Their first stop would be in Wales, to visit Ali's parents and buy a car that they could drive down and across Europe to Slovenia.

Having bought tickets from Minneapolis to London, they arrived at the airport in Minneapolis, checked their bags, and went to the boarding gate, where they discovered that Nathan's wallet—with most of his documents and cash—was missing. They went through their belongings, but to no avail. They hurried to the lost-and-found counter, but the wallet was not there.

With their boarding time rapidly approaching, they searched through their carry-on luggage one more time without success. Finally, since they still had their passports and tickets and their check-in luggage was somewhere between the counter and the plane, they decided to go on, concluding that the wallet had been stolen.

Their sense of loss and violation bothered them on their flight to England, but when they arrived in Wales, they went ahead with their plans. Nathan bought a car and planned the trip to Slovenia's capital city of Ljubljana.

The plan went awry when Nathan could not get a British driver's license in time to go. Still, they pressed on with determination and finally received good news: A friend would be driving from Wales through Ljubljana and on to Croatia. He would be glad to take them.

Within days, a small group of Christians packed two cars—one with people, the other with luggage—and headed across Europe. Everything went beautifully until they reached Ljubljana, when the driver with the luggage—instead of stopping as he should have—headed straight for Croatia without looking back until he reached the coastal city of Crikvenica. They had no choice but to follow him to the same destination, where they could retrieve their bags and return to Ljubljana.

Once in Crikvenica, they were taken to Life Center International, a ministry that brings together traumatized people and heals their wounds through friendship and the gospel.

Nathan and Ali were impressed with the ministry and learned that people with their gifts, training, and experience were needed. They soon found themselves accepting a call to join the staff. They finally understood that God had allowed everything to go wrong so it could all turn out right.

They thanked God for His guidance and were doubly blessed when—upon returning to Minneapolis—they recovered Nathan's wallet from the lost-and-found counter with money, credit cards, documents, and all.

Their ministry in the Balkans continues to grow in strategic ways, and their experience reminds us that when we commit our lives to Christ, He assumes responsibility for us and brings things together for the fulfillment of His plan. If only we would express our thanks to God for His provision—before and after it materializes—we would also be blessed.

WHAT IF THINGS DON'T TURN OUT RIGHT?

Experiences like the ones I have recorded here make us think that God has a happy ending for every situation. We longingly wish that were true, but sometimes it isn't. Sometimes things start wrong, go wrong, and end wrong, and sometimes Christians misinterpret Romans 8:28:

> *"And we know that in all things God works for the good of those who love him, who have been called according to his purpose."*

This is a wonderful affirmation that encourages us in our walk with Him. However, I don't think it means that for every bad experience we go through, God has a good one in store to make up for it. It does not mean that God owes us something special to make up for every loss He allows us to suffer.

That's not the point or the promise of the verse. God is not playing a game of rewards and punishments. He has a higher and more important purpose for the things that He allows to come our way. It's found in the next verse:

"For those God foreknew he also predestined to be conformed to the likeness of his Son, that he might be the firstborn among many brothers" (ROMANS 8:29).

God uses both positive and negative experiences to reproduce in us the qualities so evident in the life of Jesus. The purpose mentioned in Romans 8:28 is revealed in verse 29: He wants to conform us to the likeness of His Son!

I once thought that if we loved and obeyed God, we would be spared the pain and sorrow that others face. Then I remembered the suffering of Jesus and was startled by a text that implies that suffering was as essential to Him as it is to us:

"Although he was a son, he learned obedience from what he suffered and, once made perfect, he became the source of eternal salvation for all who obey him" (HEBREWS 5:8–9).

I knew that Jesus was never disobedient, so I wondered why He had to learn to obey. It must have been because His obedience became very costly. As He faced the cross He would ask to have the "cup" of suffering removed. But then, strengthened by God, He would pray, " 'Not my will, but yours be done' " (Luke 22:42). He understands our suffering and knows how to care for us and strengthen us when we feel pain.

Facing adversity is so important to spiritual growth that Paul wrote, "We also rejoice in our sufferings, because we know that suffering produces perseverance; perseverance, character; and character, hope" (Romans 5:3–4).

We develop maturity, strength, stamina, and courage by facing difficulties and making hard choices. If we never suffer, we might remain superficial and unprepared to face the future.

I'm not saying that God sends all suffering our way or that all suffering is good for us. I am saying that God bestows benefits upon us through the difficulties we endure. If we accept God's purpose of making us like Jesus, we can thank Him when circumstances come out well and even when they don't. I have been through experiences that I would not want to go through again, but neither would I want to be without the precious lessons I learned from them.

THANKING GOD FOR WHO HE IS

More important than thanking God for what He does is learning to thank and praise Him for who He is—even when we see nothing visible for which to thank Him.

God has many qualities for which He should be thanked, but of all His qualities, the Bible suggests one quality more frequently than all the others: *We should always give thanks to God that He is good, a God of unfailing love!*

> *"Enter his gates with thanksgiving and his courts with praise; give thanks to him and praise his name. For the LORD is good and his love endures forever; his faithfulness continues through all generations"* (PSALM 100:4–5).

God will never stop loving us. He will never fail us. How blessed we are to know our Savior and Lord, to trust Him and call upon

Him. Let us thank God for who He is; for what He does; and for the fact that everything He is, He wants to be to each of us in a very personal way.

I like to start each day with a fresh pot of coffee and a time alone with God. My prayer time usually begins with a couple of satisfying sips and these words: "Heavenly Father, I come into Your loving, holy presence in the name of Jesus, and I thank You for the many blessings You pour out on me and upon my family. I don't have adequate words to express my gratitude to You."

This morning I read Psalm 145 with its wonderful affirmations of God's character:

> *The Lord is great and most worthy of praise* (V. 3).
> *The Lord is gracious and compassionate* (V. 8).
> *The Lord is good to all* (V. 9).
> *The Lord is righteous in all His ways* (V. 17).
> *The Lord is near to all who call on Him* (V. 18).

I hope to always maintain an attitude of gratitude when I know things are going right and when I'm not so sure they are; when I understand what's happening and when I don't have a clue. Because God has provided and He always will…because

He is there for me and He will never fail…because He knows, He cares, He loves, He promises, He fulfills…I always want to give thanks to God.

Always.

"WHATEVER IS TRUE...
NOBLE...RIGHT...
PURE...LOVELY...
ADMIRABLE...
EXCELLENT...
PRAISEWORTHY...
THINK ABOUT
SUCH THINGS."

PHILIPPIANS 4:8

LET HIGHER THINKING
KEEP YOU FROM SINKING

IN DAY-TO-DAY LIFE THERE are things we can choose
and things we can't. Someone once said, "The difference
between friends and relatives is that you can choose your
friends." It's nice when our relatives are also our close friends.

We can also choose our thoughts, and if we want peace of
heart and mind, we need to choose the thoughts as carefully
as we choose friends. We need to choose those thoughts so
consistently that they become our friends.

Think about it: The crowning work of God's creation is the
human race. God created us in His own image. The abilities
that most distinguish us from the rest of creation are our
ability to think and our ability to choose. Since we have these

God-given abilities, we need to think about what we choose and choose what we think about.

Higher thinking keeps us from sinking…into discouragement, despair, defeat, and destruction. Wrong thinking robs us of peace of heart and mind.

UPBEAT THOUGHTS
OR DOWNWARD SLIDES?

In the book of Isaiah we read, "You will keep in perfect peace him whose mind is steadfast, because he trusts in you" (Isaiah 26:3).

Perfect peace comes from a steadfast mind. That sounds easy enough in normal times, but when we are going through agitated, agonizing times, a steadfast mind is not so easy to achieve. It requires determination, discipline, and faith.

Imagine what thoughts occurred to Paul during his prison experience. Without that mental toughness, he might have slipped into despondency. Yet we see in Paul an enormous determination to stay "on top" spiritually, mentally, and emotionally. His determination to think positively gives him the right to tell us to choose noble, right, pure, lovely, admirable, excellent, and praiseworthy thoughts—especially when we are going through trials that would otherwise make us think in negative, resentful, and self-destructive ways.

Paul trained himself to think in positive, godly ways as evidenced by this sampler of his "higher thinking," found in Philippians:

"He who began a good work in you will carry it on to completion until the day of Christ Jesus" (1:6).

"What has happened to me has really served to advance the gospel" (1:12).

"Christ is preached…. I rejoice" (1:18).

"I consider everything a loss compared to the surpassing greatness of knowing Christ Jesus my Lord" (3:8).

"I can do everything through him who gives me strength" (4:13).

"My God will meet all your needs according to his glorious riches in Christ Jesus" (4:19).

Just repeating these verses can lift a downcast spirit. You can almost feel Paul's determination coming into your heart and mind. What a wonderful way to think when you are suffering!

David was equally determined to think uplifting thoughts. Forced to move from cave to cave, fleeing the mad obsession of King Saul who sought to kill him, David made enormous sacrifices in order to avoid touching "the Lord's anointed." David's advice for a healthy mind is stated in Psalm 1:1–2:

> *"Blessed is the man who does not walk in the counsel of the wicked or stand in the way of sinners or sit in the seat of mockers. But his delight is in the law of the LORD, and on his law he meditates day and night."*

David shows his mind-set in statements like these from Psalm 119:

—I WILL MEDITATE ON YOUR WAYS.

—I WILL MEDITATE ON YOUR PROMISES.

—I WILL MEDITATE ON YOUR DECREES.

—I WILL MEDITATE ON YOUR WONDERS.

—I WILL MEDITATE ON YOUR PRECEPTS.

—I WILL MEDITATE ON YOUR LAW.

—I WILL MEDITATE ON YOUR STATUTES.

—I WILL MEDITATE ON YOUR WORKS.

In contrast, the Bible tells us that we should not think in unhealthy ways:

—DO NOT THINK EVIL OF ONE ANOTHER.

—DO NOT THINK DISPARAGINGLY OF YOURSELF.

—DO NOT THINK TOO HIGHLY OF YOURSELF.

—DO NOT THINK ABOUT HOW TO GRATIFY FLESHLY DESIRES.

HIGHER THINKING AND BETTER SELF-TALK

The late author, minister, and psychologist Dr. William Backus made an enlightening statement: "I have come to realize what Jesus meant when He said, 'The truth will set you free.' Along with freedom from sin, I believe He meant to proclaim freedom from negative thoughts and their effects on our bodies."

In *Telling Yourself the Truth*[1] and other books, Dr. Backus proposes "Truth Therapy." He suggests we identify "misbeliefs" in our "self-talk" and learn to substitute them with positive statements of truth based on the Word of God—when we speak to others and when we speak to ourselves!

"The weapons we fight with," says the Bible in 2 Corinthians 10:4–5, "are not the weapons of the world. On the contrary, they have divine power to demolish strongholds. We demolish arguments and every pretension that sets itself up against the knowledge of God, and we take captive every thought to make it obedient to Christ."

If we're serious about winning the battle for the mind, we must replace hurtful thoughts with healthy ones. We must make room in our lives for prayer and for the inspired thoughts of the Bible. Prayer empowers us to discern and displace lies. The Bible gives us truth to replace them.

When Satan tempted Jesus, Jesus made use of God's Word to resist the devil's approaches. Three times Satan appeared. Three times Jesus resisted him, saying, " 'It is written...,' " quoting God's Word (see Luke 4:4, 8, 12). Later Jesus told His disciples, " 'Watch and pray so that you will not fall into temptation' " (Matthew 26:41).

HIGHER THOUGHTS ABOUT GOD

When I was thirteen years old, I was given a catechism book to study. I have never forgotten how it started:

Q. What is the highest and most important knowledge?
A. The highest and most important knowledge is to know God and His Son Jesus Christ.

This affirmation is supported by a biblical statement that tells us what God thinks about the value of knowledge:

"This is what the LORD says: 'Let not the wise man boast of his wisdom or the strong man boast

of his strength or the rich man boast of his riches,
but let him who boasts boast about this: that he
understands and knows me, that I am the LORD,
who exercises kindness, justice and righteousness on
earth, for in these I delight,' declares the LORD"
(JEREMIAH 9:23–24).

Our greatest source of strength is God Himself—our knowledge of Him, our intimacy with Him, and our awareness of His presence in our lives. We need insight into His ways, His Word, and His will, and we need to keep those things in mind.

Some statements we hear about God could distort our knowledge of Him. Descriptions of His transcendence make Him seem austere, impassive, and distant. Words about His immanence make Him seem like little more than a "souped-up" version of man. Some picture Him as a stern God who would be hard to love, serve, trust, or recommend to others. Some see Him as permissive, grandfatherly—even wimpy.

The Bible reveals God as loving and holy, a God who—when we get a clear look at Him—is easy to respect and love.

Since God is…

GOOD:	He wants what is best for me.
	He loves to bless me.
WISE:	He knows what is best for me.
	His plans are better than mine.
HOLY:	He wants to keep me clean.
	He will never do anything wrong.
POWERFUL:	He can do what is best for me.
	Nothing is too hard for Him.
FAITHFUL:	He promises what is best for me.
	He keeps His word.
PATIENT:	He waits for me to accept what is best for me.
	His timing is certain.
JUST:	He does what is right for me.
	His ways and works are perfect.
CARING:	He feels my pain and suffers when I do.
	He is always with me.

God is, above all, a God of a multifaceted love who meets all of our human needs. His love is…

INFINITE:	Nothing can be added to it or taken from it.
INDISCRIMINATE:	It places equal value upon each of us.
UNCONDITIONAL:	It is unaffected by efforts to earn it or reject it.
PERSONAL:	It singles us out and calls us by name.
UNIVERSAL:	It reaches out to everyone, everywhere.
HEALING:	It soothes our heartaches and makes us well.
FORGIVING:	It takes us in when we turn to Him.
VICTORIOUS:	It defeats the power of sin and death.
ETERNAL:	It never leaves us or forsakes us. It never ends.
RELENTLESS:	It never gives up on us.

Some difficult experiences we go through insinuate that these statements may not be true or do not apply to us. We may think that God is not blessing us or is punishing us or has forgotten us or doesn't care.

But these statements come from God's Word and reflect what God wants us to think about Him. They are the thoughts about Him that we need to choose because they are true, noble, right, pure, lovely—the thoughts that will strengthen us through our most troubling times.

HIGHER THOUGHTS ABOUT GOD'S WILL

God wants us as friends, and He wants to equip us for life, ministry, and achievement. We were created in God's image, and although He has no plans to make us into gods or angels, He does want us to fully develop into the persons He made us to be. He does not see His creation as a mass of humanity. He sees us as individuals, gives value to us, and has plans for us.

GOD OUR FATHER/CREATOR has prepared us to do good works—and has prepared good works for us to do. He made us with the ability to do those works in cooperation with Him.

GOD OUR REDEEMER, Jesus Christ, forgives our foolish refusal to surrender to His will and, once we surrender, restores our ability to fulfill His plan so that we can be all He created us to be and do all He created us to do.

GOD OUR ENABLER, the Holy Spirit, empowers us to be effective workers and witnesses under His call and direction. When we know who we are in Christ and what our calling is, we receive grace to fulfill His plan for us.

Some Christians are afraid to embrace God's will. Their inadequate or faulty vision of God makes His will seem difficult or unpleasant. The opposite is true. I recently found myself in complete agreement with someone who said, "What God wants for us is what we would want for ourselves if we just had better sense."

Although we may never fully comprehend God's will, scripture says that we can experience it when we follow the instructions laid down in His Word:

> *"I urge you, brothers, in view of God's mercy, to offer your bodies as living sacrifices, holy and pleasing to God— this is your spiritual act of worship. Do not conform any longer to the pattern of this world, but be transformed by the renewing of your mind. Then you will be able to test*

and approve what God's will is—His good, pleasing and perfect will" (ROMANS 12:1–2).

. . . .

This text gives us simple instructions that are easy to understand, though not always easy to follow:

OFFER YOUR BODY [SELF] TO GOD. To experience God's will, we must be willing to *do* His will—not because we understand every detail of it, but because we trust in His character and know that He knows, wants, and does what is best for us. With that confidence, we surrender our will to His.

DO NOT CONFORM TO THIS WORLD. The changing values of our culture can make a negative impact on us. In many cases, the culture affects the church more than the church affects the culture. We must not allow ourselves to be unduly shaped by the world in which we live but instead allow God to use us to make a positive impact upon it.

BE TRANSFORMED BY THE RENEWING OF YOUR MIND. We must not withdraw from the world or let it overpower us. We must be aware of what is said and done around us but live by the truths and values taught in

God's Word. Jesus said: " 'Love the Lord your God with all your heart and with all your soul and *with all your mind*' " (Matthew 22:37, italics added).

A renewed mind, marked by higher levels of thinking and unfolding spiritual vision, energizes and renews us. When we give ourselves to God, resist the offers of this world, and renew our minds to align them with God, we're on track with Him to experience His good, acceptable, and perfect will.

HIGHER THOUGHTS
ABOUT OURSELVES

Once Paul shares the three steps to experience God's will, he addresses our need to have a humble yet confident view of ourselves, our abilities, and our need to trust in God's empowering to do His will.

> *"Do not think of yourself more highly than you ought, but rather think of yourself with sober judgment, in accordance with the measure of faith God has given you"* (ROMANS 12:3).

Sometimes our worst thoughts have to do with ourselves—who we are, and how much or how little we think we are worth. Many of these thoughts have come to us from those closest to us—parents, siblings, spouses, and friends:

—YOU'RE NO GOOD.

—YOU'LL NEVER AMOUNT TO ANYTHING.

—DON'T SET YOUR GOALS SO HIGH.

—DON'T TRY; YOU WON'T SUCCEED.

—NO ONE CARES ABOUT YOU.

—IT'S TOO LATE FOR YOU.

—WHAT MAKES YOU THINK YOU CAN DO IT?

—YOU'RE NOT QUALIFIED.

—YOU'RE TOO YOUNG (OR TOO OLD).

These untrue or distorted statements are "strongholds" that Satan uses to prevent us from becoming the persons God intends for us to be and from doing the things God intends for us to do. If we accept these ideas as true, we are defeated. We must get rid of them!

Look again at Paul's words. They will help us think healthy, biblical thoughts about ourselves.

"We are God's workmanship, created in Christ Jesus to do good works, which God prepared in advance for us to do"
(EPHESIANS 2:10).

GOD GIVES ME VALUE!

When I feel useless, hopeless, helpless, worthless;
Rejected, dejected, disconnected, unprotected;
When I make mistakes, get bad breaks,
Wonder what difference my life makes;
—I think on these things:

MY VALUE COMES FROM GOD—not from what I look like, what I can do, what I possess, how I behave, or my standing in society. I am made in God's image. God cares for me, invests in me, believes in me, and has a plan for me.

MY USEFUL VALUE IS DIMINISHED BY SIN. When I disobey God, I frustrate His purposes, fall short of His standards, and miss out on His plans for me. I lose contact with Him, and I lose understanding about who He made me to be.

MY TRUE VALUE IS REDEEMED BY CHRIST. God loves me just as I am, but He loves me too much to leave me as I am. He sent His Son, the Lord Jesus Christ, to redeem me, restore me, redirect me, and renew me. What price did Jesus pay? His life, His blood—that's how much He treasures me.

MY VALUE IS RENEWED AS I WALK WITH HIM.

I accept Christ; He accepts me. I repent of my sins; He forgives me. My old life dies with Him; new life begins with Him. I live in Him; He lives in me. I trust Him; and, believe it or not, He trusts me.

GOD WILL FULFILL HIS PLANS FOR ME. He has

prepared me to do good works and He has prepared good works for me to do. He will not give up on His plans. He will not give up on me. He will finish the good work He began in me.

I TRUST IN GOD. Nothing separates me from Him—

not death, life, angels, demons, past, present, future, height, depth—nothing! He is with me to help me and guide me. He will never leave me and I will never leave Him. He will always guide me and I will always follow Him. He will always sustain me and I will never fear. I will be the person God made me to be, and I will do what God gives me to do.

HIGHER THOUGHTS ABOUT OTHERS

Paul's statement helps us see not only our own value in God's plan; we also see the value of others. He does not say, "*I am* His workmanship"; he says, "*We are* His workmanship."

This statement is true for everyone. We are all His workmanship. He has a plan for every person. He cares for each of us. That being the case, there are several considerations to make with regard to other people:

—WE ARE ALL OF EQUAL VALUE BEFORE GOD.

—WE ARE EXPRESSIONS OF GOD'S LOVE FOR DIVERSITY.

—WE DO NOT HAVE TO ENVY OR IMITATE OTHERS.

—WE DO NOT HAVE TO COMPARE OURSELVES WITH OTHERS.

—WE DO NOT HAVE TO COMPETE WITH OTHERS.

—WE SHOULD NOT FEEL INFERIOR OR SUPERIOR TO OTHERS.

—WE CAN WORK WITH OTHERS IN CHRIST'S KINGDOM.

—WE CAN RESPECT AND HONOR THE DIGNITY OF ALL PEOPLE.

—AS WE SERVE OTHER PEOPLE, WE SERVE GOD.

—WE SHOULD SEEK TO BRING PEOPLE TO CHRIST.

—WE SHOULD SHARE GENEROUSLY WITH ALL PEOPLE.

As we relate to brothers and sisters in the body of Christ, we see that we have more similarities than differences. The question is not, Am I called to serve God? The question is, Where do I fit in God's plan, to which everyone is called? God calls us to work together in the body of Christ. He calls us to help each other follow Christ more faithfully, serve Christ more diligently, and share Christ more effectively.

Each of us has a part to play, and we have the gifts that empower us to play our part. Our value is enhanced when we find our place and join with others in a way that multiplies the effectiveness of what they do and what we do *together*.

Giving ourselves completely to God, refusing to be molded by our culture, and seeking transformation through renewing our minds, let us choose thoughts that are true, noble, right, pure, lovely, admirable, excellent, and praiseworthy—higher thinking that will keep us from sinking.

"WHATEVER YOU HAVE LEARNED... FROM ME... PUT IT INTO PRACTICE."

PHILIPPIANS 4:9

DON'T LOSE IT.
DON'T ABUSE IT.
DON'T FAIL TO USE IT!

THE ACQUISITION OF INFORMATION does not make it part of our lives—we all know that. It becomes part of us when we consistently apply it to our lives and establish new patterns of thinking, speaking, and acting.

Paul wanted his instruction to the Philippians to be more than accumulated knowledge. He wanted those early Christians to assimilate his teaching. So he insisted:

"Whatever you have learned or received or heard from me, or seen in me—put it into practice" (PHILIPPIANS 4:9).

James also insisted that we put God's Word into practice and described what we are like when we fail to do so in James 1:22–24:

> *"Do not merely listen to the word, and so deceive yourselves.*
> *Do what it says. Anyone who listens to the word but does not*
> *do what it says is like a man who looks at his face in a mirror*
> *and, after looking at himself, goes away and immediately forgets*
> *what he looks like."*

In the Bible we get a vision of God and a vision of ourselves. We see ourselves as God sees us. We gain a sense of identity that is founded upon God's Word. James warns us that unless we *act* on what we see, the vision we get from God for our lives will soon be forgotten.

Jesus, too, spoke of the negative effects of taking in right information and failing to act on it, in Luke 6:46–49:

> *"Why do you call me, 'Lord, Lord,' and do not do what I say?*
> *I will show you what he is like who comes to me and hears my*
> *words and puts them into practice. He is like a man building*
> *a house, who dug down deep and laid the foundation on rock.*
> *When a flood came, the torrent struck that house but could not*
> *shake it, because it was well built.*

But the one who hears my words and does not put them into practice is like a man who built a house on the ground without a foundation. The moment the torrent struck that house, it collapsed and its destruction was complete."

We have already observed the disciples in the storm on the Sea of Galilee. The passage above describes another storm, this one beating against a house. This passage warns us that a house built on a shaky foundation will not withstand the fury of the storm. When the winds blow and the rushing floodwaters are unleashed, the ground will erode beneath the house, and it will collapse. When the foundation is solid, the storm will not wash the house away. The house will stand firm.

A life built on obedience to God's Word will also withstand the storm.

During the recent storms I have been through, I have sought to follow God's recipe for inner peace, and He has given me strength and peace in the midst of the storm. I have asked the Lord almost daily to help me make my heart completely His, and I have seen the floodwaters carry away things that were too important to me and are not so important now.

INFORMATION OR TRANSFORMATION?

Jesus, Paul, and James all knew that they were not really teaching unless someone was learning. They spoke so that people would learn and their lives would be changed. They taught in a way that demanded a response.

D. L. Moody added his voice to the biblical trio when he said, "The Bible wasn't given for our information, but for our transformation."

What will you do with this information about rejoicing, gentleness, anxiety, prayer, thankfulness, and higher thinking? Will it be mere information, or will it bring transformation? Will you apply these biblical principles to your life until they become a strong foundation on which you can stand?

When you start the day complaining, you find something wrong with nearly everything that happens that day. When you start out angry, everything becomes a source of irritation. When you are impatient with one person, you may become impatient with yourself, as well, and treat everyone poorly. When you begin with anxiety, the events of the day seem to confirm that your future looks dreary.

You lose your sense of hope and happiness. You lose your peace. Soon you are thinking, *What's the use of praying? What do*

I have to rejoice about and be thankful for? Peace?—not
with the job I have, the spouse I have, the boss I have!

It takes courage and determination to put God's Word into practice, but it's worth the effort. The more you obey, the more you want to obey. The more determination you exercise, the stronger you become. Speak and act with determination: I *will* rejoice. I *will* be gentle. I *will not* worry. I *will* pray. I *will* give thanks. I *will* think higher thoughts. I *will* be positive. I *will* trust God. God *will* help me do what I need to do!

GOD'S WORD FOR EVERY SITUATION

The longest chapter in the Bible is devoted to expressing the value of reading and obeying God's Word. The psalmist's love for God's Word is summed up in this verse: "Your word is a lamp to my feet and a light for my path" (Psalm 119:105).

How can we get maximum benefits from Bible reading? Many of us need to start by asking forgiveness for neglecting God's Word and then work on a planned approach that includes the following determinations:

1. I WILL READ WITH EXPECTANCY. I believe that God has something to say to me, and I'll read until I find it. "Open my eyes to see the wonderful truths in your instructions" (Psalm 119:18 NLT).

2. I WILL ASK QUESTIONS. What does God want to tell me in this passage? What does it teach me about God? About Jesus? About me? About His will? Is there a command to obey? A promise to claim? An example to follow? How do these truths apply to my life? My family? My job? My studies? My church?

3. I WILL READ THE PASSAGE SEVERAL TIMES. Repetition will help me understand. I will use the Bible's cross-references to find verses that deal with the same subject or related ones. I will compare them, make notes on them, and see how they complement each other.

4. I WILL MEDITATE ON THE WORDS. It's better to understand, absorb, and apply a short passage than to read hurriedly, with superficial understanding of the text. (See Psalm 1.)

5. I WILL MEMORIZE VERSES AND REFERENCES. "Remember my words with your whole being" (Deuteronomy 11:18). God's words will strengthen me if I have them in my memory. I will set aside time to acquire the spiritual resources I need.

6. I WILL READ FROM COVER TO COVER. I need a complete and balanced look at the Bible's major themes. "All Scripture is God-breathed and is useful for teaching, rebuking, correcting and training in righteousness" (2 Timothy 3:16).

7. I WILL READ WITH A DETERMINATION TO OBEY. "Do what God's word says.... Happy is the one who studies God's law.... He listens to God's teaching and does not forget what he heard.... He obeys God's teaching...." (see James 1:22 NIV and Psalm 119:1–3 NCV).

8. I WILL LEARN AND APPLY APPROPRIATE VERSES. Specific problems need specific solutions. The following verses provide appropriate words for difficult moments in life:

WHEN I FEEL...

ABANDONED—"The LORD will fulfill his purpose for me; your love, O LORD, endures forever—do not abandon the works of your hands" (Psalm 138:8).

AFRAID—"Do not fear, for I am with you; do not be dismayed, for I am your God" (Isaiah 41:10).

ALONE—" 'Never will I leave you; never will I forsake you' " (Hebrews 13:5).

ANGRY—"Refrain from anger and turn from wrath; do not fret—it leads only to evil" (Psalm 37:8).

ANGUISHED—" 'My grace is sufficient for you, for my power is made perfect in weakness' " (2 Corinthians 12:9).

ANXIOUS—"Do not be anxious about anything, but in everything, by prayer and petition, with thanksgiving, present your requests to God" (Philippians 4:6).

ASHAMED—"No one whose hope is in you will ever be put to shame" (Psalm 25:3).

ATTACKED—"I will contend with those who contend with you" (Isaiah 49:25).

CONDEMNED—"There is now no condemnation for those who are in Christ Jesus" (Romans 8:1).

CONFUSED—"I will lead the blind by ways they have not known…. I will guide them; I will turn the darkness into light… and make rough places smooth" (Isaiah 42:16).

DEPLETED—"He gives strength to the weary and increases the power of the weak…. Those who hope in the LORD will renew their strength. They will soar on wings like eagles; they will run and not grow weary, they will walk and not be faint" (Isaiah 40:29, 31).

DOUBTFUL—"Trust in the LORD with all your heart and lean not on your own understanding; in all your ways acknowledge him, and he will make your paths straight" (Proverbs 3:5–6).

DISCOURAGED—"He who began a good work in you will carry it on to completion until the day of Christ Jesus" (Philippians 1:6).

FEARFUL OF PEOPLE—" 'The Lord is my helper; I will not be afraid. What can man do to me?' " (Hebrews 13:6).

FORGOTTEN—" 'Can a mother forget the baby at her breast? ...I [the Lord] will not forget you!' " (Isaiah 49:15).

GUILTY—"If we confess our sins, he is faithful and just and will forgive us our sins and purify us from all unrighteousness" (1 John 1:9).

HURTING—"As a mother comforts her child, so will I [the Lord] comfort you" (Isaiah 66:13). "Praise be to the God and Father of our Lord Jesus Christ, the Father of compassion and the God of all comfort, who comforts us in all our troubles, so that we can comfort those in any trouble with the comfort we ourselves have received from God" (2 Corinthians 1:3–4).

INFERIOR—"God chose the foolish things of the world to shame the wise; God chose the weak things of the world to shame the strong" (1 Corinthians 1:27).

LONELY—"God has said, 'Never will I leave you; never will I forsake you.' So we say with confidence, 'The Lord is my helper; I will not be afraid. What can man do to me?' " (Hebrews 13:5–6).

OVERCONFIDENT—" 'I am the vine; you are the branches. If a man remains in me and I in him, he will bear much fruit; apart from me you can do nothing' " (John 15:5).

PROUD—" 'God opposes the proud but gives grace to the humble' " (1 Peter 5:5).

REJECTED—"I have chosen you and have not rejected you" (Isaiah 41:9).

RESENTFUL—"Be kind and compassionate to one another, forgiving each other, just as in Christ God forgave you" (Ephesians 4:32).

UNABLE—"I can do everything through him who gives me strength" (Philippians 4:13).

UNAPPRECIATED—" 'This is the one I esteem: he who is humble and contrite in spirit, and trembles at my word' " (Isaiah 66:2).

UNCERTAIN—" 'I know the plans I have for you,' declares the LORD, 'plans to prosper you and not to harm you, plans to give you hope and a future' " (Jeremiah 29:11).

UNLOVED—" 'I have loved you with an everlasting love; I have drawn you with loving-kindness. I will build you up again and you will be rebuilt' " (Jeremiah 31:3–4).

UNPROTECTED—"If you make the Most High your dwelling...then no harm will befall you" (Psalm 91:9–10).

WEAK—"God is the strength of my heart and my portion forever" (Psalm 73:26).

WORRIED—" 'Do not worry about tomorrow, for tomorrow will worry about itself. Each day has enough trouble of its own' " (Matthew 6:34).

WORTHLESS—"For we are God's workmanship, created in Christ Jesus to do good works, which God prepared in advance for us to do" (Ephesians 2:10).

PREPARING THE SOIL
OF OUR HEARTS

We've seen two biblical metaphors about receiving the Word of God and obeying its message—the foundation and the mirror. Let's consider one more—the sowing of good seed (Matthew 13:3–9; Luke 8:4–8).

Jesus spoke of four different types of soil upon which the seed might fall: *beaten-down soil* located along the path, *thin soil* located in rocky places, *choked soil* located in thorny places, and *good soil* located in productive places.

The challenge is not only to find good soil where we can sow gospel seeds; it's also to make sure that our hearts are prepared to receive God's Word every day. By keeping in touch with God and by obeying the truth we receive, we keep our hearts like freshly plowed soil. God's truth has a wonderful and powerful effect upon us.

If we fail to apply the words we have heard, the soil becomes hardened and the seed either is stolen from us or choked out by the weeds that accumulate, or the soil is too hard for the seed to germinate and produce fruit.

When I was a student, my teachers used to say, "Obedience precedes revelation." Jesus said essentially the same thing in different words: "If anyone chooses to do God's will, he will find out whether my teaching comes from God or whether I speak on my own" (John 7:17). We must not annul the blessing of having God's Word by failing to apply and obey it. We must make it ours by putting it to use in our lives today.

"AND THE PEACE OF GOD,
WHICH TRANSCENDS
ALL UNDERSTANDING,
WILL GUARD YOUR HEARTS
AND YOUR MINDS IN
CHRIST JESUS....
AND THE GOD OF PEACE
WILL BE WITH YOU."

PHILIPPIANS 4:7, 9

INCREASE YOUR PEACE

THE PRESCRIPTION FOR PEACE IS NOW
COMPLETE: Make a choice to rejoice. Make up your
mind to be kind. Don't sweat. Don't fret. Don't get upset.
Make a way to pray every day. Make gratitude your attitude.
Let higher thinking keep you from sinking. Don't
lose it. Don't abuse it. Don't fail to use it!

It's time to see the results:

> *"The peace of God, which transcends all understanding, will
> guard your hearts and your minds in Christ Jesus.... And the
> God of peace will be with you"* (PHILIPPIANS 4:7, 9).

How fascinating that Paul puts it both ways: the peace of God and the God of peace. They are inseparable. To have one, you must have the other. The recipe includes several ingredients, but the essential one is Jesus Himself! To find peace we must *look* to Jesus, *trust* in Jesus, and *abide* in Jesus. We can take all the steps and miss the point unless Christ is at the center of it all. Christ must be in the first step, the last step, and every step in between—but we must not fail to take the steps!

Oswald Chambers wrote: "There are times when our peace is based simply on our own ignorance. But when we are awakened to the realities of life, true inner peace is impossible unless it is received from Jesus."[1]

PEACE ONLY FROM JESUS

I have shared from my recent experience about when the peace I had known became elusive. I must tell you a little more. Writing this book was not as peaceful a job as I thought it would be. It was complicated when my church leadership team moved in a direction that I could not go. Although I agreed with many changes that were made, I disagreed with others. I tried to stay on the team and make a case for alternative paths, but my efforts failed and I saw no other option but to resign.

The process was extremely painful both for me and for the other team members, as well—especially the pastor, a godly man whom I hold in high esteem and with true affection. What brought about my decision to leave was not a dislike for him or anyone but because of our divergent views on ministry.

After submitting my resignation, I spoke with him about that painful time in our lives. I remarked that it was ironic to be writing about peace at such a time.

His answer surprised me: "It sounds like a God thing."

I wondered how that could be. Shouldn't a book about peace come from tranquillity rather than turbulence? What made me think that I could write about peace when I felt so troubled? When I was close to abandoning the project, I went back to the first chapter:

> "The winning entry was painted by an artist who used bold, dark strokes to portray a violent storm with fierce wind, driving rain, and jagged lightning. Lines converged on a cleft in an enormous rock where—protected from the elements and completely undisturbed—perched a bright, irrepressible bird."

I wanted to feel more like that bird (and less like the worm that nourished it). I kept on writing and discovered that working through the pain and the pages together was good for me—especially writing "Make Up Your Mind to Be Kind," the chapter that Dolly said I wrote for myself.

When the pastor suggested that our disagreement was like that of Barnabas and Paul, I remembered that Barnabas had encouraged, mentored, and worked with Paul until a disagreement divided them. Then I read through the events that took place in their relationship:

THEY WERE CALLED TO BE TOGETHER IN MINISTRY. "While they were worshiping the Lord and fasting, the Holy Spirit said, 'Set apart for me Barnabas and Saul for the work to which I have called them' " (Acts 13:2).

THEY WERE BLESSED TOGETHER IN MINISTRY. "So Paul and Barnabas spent considerable time there, speaking boldly for the Lord, who confirmed the message of his grace by enabling them to do miraculous signs and wonders" (Acts 14:3).

THEY DISAGREED AND WENT INTO SEPARATE MINISTRIES. "They had such a sharp disagreement that they

parted company. Barnabas took Mark and sailed for
Cyprus" (Acts 15:39).

The separation must have left both of them with regrets,
but they found the space they needed to develop their
ministries. When I saw that God didn't vindicate one and
castigate the other, I was strengthened in my decision to resign.
It was also helpful to consider the question raised in Amos 3:3:
"Can two walk together, except they be agreed?" (KJV).

I was the one who had disagreed with the majority, the one
not accepting things, the one raising issues, the one who should
have been more patient and gentle. I was the one who had to
apologize more than once.

Sometimes during that period I allowed my mind to follow
the arguments to their conclusions. When I did, I would lose my
peace and the sense of God's approval. But each time I followed
the "prescription for peace" that forms the basis for this book,
God's peace would return.

My decision to leave did not completely resolve things
for me. I continued to think about the situation. I actually let
go of the issues several times and picked them up again. I
knew that I couldn't continue that way and finally crossed a
barrier that allowed me to hear Jesus speak: "Peace be still,"

as He did in Mark 4:39. He enabled me to let go of my issues and allow Him to bring me through the troubled waters safely to shore.

I can say now that both the trials we went through and the decision to leave have been good for Dolly and me. Our experiences have helped us gain understanding into the trials people go through and have enabled us to minister encouragement to them. We're more sensitive to the needs of Christians who struggle with issues that rob them of their peace, and we're much more compassionate than we were before.

When, for instance, a friend called to talk about a conflict he was going through, I could identify with him and minister to him in a way that I couldn't have done before. I was able to offer words of understanding and encouragement.

When another friend was released from a ministry that he had helped to build, he felt betrayed. In the midst of his grief, he learned exactly how he should handle his feelings. When I shared Paul's "prescription" with him, he wrote:

> It's as if for the past four months, I already had your words with me. I have followed, and continue to follow, each step you have described—not so much in search of peace, but because it's the way I know I have to walk.

For me, at least in the beginning, the hardest part was to keep my thoughts in line. Because I tend to be a bit melancholic, it was easy for me to feel that I'd been mistreated and to feel sorry for myself.

I found that whenever that started, unless I changed my thoughts and attitude immediately, I would find myself desiring that those who fired me would be unsuccessful in their ministry.

I thank God that those thoughts rarely occur now. I'm leaving not only with peace of mind but desiring with all my heart that God's blessing will rest upon those who dismissed me."

God's peace was present with my friend in a new way, enabling him to move on and leave a powerful witness to God's grace as he did so. For me, that peace has come to calm the storm and enable me to address this subject in a more rational yet spiritual way. I have a deep sense of confidence that Christ will not only be with me in the storms of life, but that He will enable me to go through them with less pain and greater victory.

WE NEED GOD'S PRESENCE

In the midst of our struggles, we need principles, promises, practices, and prayer. But we also need God's presence—a fact that seems too obvious to state but one that begs for our attention. Some Christians say, "If I'm a believer, how can He not be with me? If I belong to Him, then He has to be with me. After all, I have His promises":

> " *'I am with you always, to the very end of the age'* "
> (MATTHEW 28:20).
> " *'Never will I leave you; never will I forsake you'* "
> (HEBREWS 13:5).

I agree. God is always with us. Yet James says, "Come near to God and he will come near to you" (James 4:8).

Is there a contradiction here? He is always with me, yet I must seek Him? He lives in me, yet I must draw near to Him?

I see no contradiction. Let me remind you of a passage I cited in chapter 3: "Do not grieve the Holy Spirit of God…. Be kind and compassionate…." (Ephesians 4:30, 32). Though He dwells in us, we can lose His comfort and anointing. We must always seek a greater sense of His presence and a greater portion of His enabling grace. We must seek the Lord even though He is always with us.

PEACE THAT TRANSCENDS UNDERSTANDING

I've heard Christians thank God that during enormous trials they experienced a special state of grace and peace, lifting them to a plain above excessive suffering. On the other hand, I've heard believers say that it was the agony of their troubles and their suffering that brought them to a deeper experience of grace. Either way, God encourages us to believe Him for a peace beyond anything that, naturally speaking, we would have the right to expect or the ability to explain.

I have had to examine God's Word and examine myself in the light of it. I've had to ask myself if I was willing to put its teachings to work. It made me deal with the issues I was facing. It has been a means of grace to me.

PERFECT PEACE IN HEAVEN

It was a cold night back in Curitiba, Brazil, when—either by dream, vision, or the effects of spicy pizza—I felt as if I was in heaven. I can't recall any visual perceptions, but I was left with two distinct impressions of the atmosphere.

The first was an immediate sense of freedom. In heaven there were no limitations. I didn't have to learn a celestial language; I already knew it. The desire to know something gave me intuitive mastery of it. And there was no need for transportation. With no earthbound body to hold me down, the mere desire to be somewhere put me there.

The second impression was an almost incredible sense of peace. In heaven, there was no anxiety or conflict. There were no tears, no fears, no pain, no sorrow. But peace was not just the absence of conflict or anxiety; it was the presence of something indescribable, incomparable, almost palpable. Thick and glorious, it could only be God. The presence of God meant peace. Heaven was permeated with it: Total peace! Absolute peace! Eternal peace!

Add to that a sense of joy—but I hesitate to say that joy was a third impression. Peace and joy seemed synonymous. How could one have so much peace and not have joy?

Paul made a statement in Romans 8:18 about the suffering...

"I consider that our present sufferings are not worth comparing with the glory that will be revealed in us."

BRINGING HEAVEN TO EARTH

Whether or not these impressions picture heaven as it truly is, heaven is the hope we treasure. How important is that hope? Jesus made a point of speaking about it in John 14:1–6 when He wanted His disciples to be at peace on earth:

> " 'Do not let your hearts be troubled. Trust in God; trust also in me. In my Father's house are many rooms; if it were not so, I would have told you. I am going there to prepare a place for you. And if I go and prepare a place for you, I will come back and take you to be with me that you also may be where I am. You know the way to the place where I am going.'
>
> Thomas said to him, 'Lord, we don't know where you are going, so how can we know the way?'
>
> Jesus answered, 'I am the way and the truth and the life. No one comes to the Father except through me.' "

In a newsletter for missionaries titled *Encouragement*,[2] Lareau Lindquist of Barnabas International wrote:

"Some years ago I was the Saturday morning preacher at a large synagogue in Toronto, Alberta, Canada. It was their regular Shabbat worship service, just days before Yom Kippur. I chose to speak on, perhaps, the favorite word of many Jews—shalom, meaning 'peace.' I spoke entirely from the Old Testament, which they call the Hebrew Bible. I told them that their Bible speaks of peace in at least three dimensions: personal inner peace, relational peace between people and between nations, and eternal peace with the Lord in His heaven. The Jews living in Israel do not yet know peace within their land, nor along its borders, but someday there will be peace.

I spoke of the peace coming from their promised Messiah, the Prince of Peace. In the Old Testament times, people found peace by looking forward to the Prince of Peace. In the New Testament and since, we find peace by looking back to Him…to Jesus, the true Prince of Peace. I told them that peace is based on a relationship between us and the Father through His Son, the Prince of Peace."

Jesus taught us to pray for peace, to work for peace, and to be guided by His peace in all the decisions we make. We are to bless people with a blessing of peace, and we are to live in anticipation of eternal peace while learning to experience greater and greater degrees of peace in this life. (See appendix for a brief biblical progression that describes the coming of lasting peace.)

Perhaps you still have not experienced this peace. Maybe, after reading these pages, you recognize that only the Lord Jesus Christ offers the peace that you have not experienced.

I urge you to put your trust in the Prince of Peace. The first peace that Jesus offers is the peace that comes when you know that your sins are forgiven and that Christ has prepared and guaranteed for you a place in the kingdom of heaven. Paul described that peace in these words in Romans 5:1–2:

> *"Therefore, since we have been justified through faith, we have peace with God through our Lord Jesus Christ, through whom we have gained access by faith into this grace in which we now stand."*

Let me remind you that God loves you just as you are, but He loves you too much to leave you as you are. He'll remake you with the power to live a life that's worthy of the person He made you to be. Trust Him! He'll take care of everything you give Him—*so give Him your life!* He'll be with you—through every storm that comes into your life.

HERE'S HOW TO DO IT NOW:

TALK TO GOD! Admit you need to change. Give up your self-destructive acts and attitudes. Ask Him to help you get sin out of your life, to fill the empty space, and to get yourself under control.

OPEN YOUR HEART. Jesus says, " 'I stand at the door and knock. If you hear my voice and open the door, I will come in' " (see Revelation 3:20). Invite Him. He'll come to you.

LET HIM GUIDE YOU. Get a Bible and read it. Pray and thank God every day. Get with people who live for God. Tell others what you are learning whenever you can.

Then…

"Let the peace of Christ rule in your hearts, since as members of one body you were called to peace. And be thankful" (COLOSSIANS 3:15).

"May the Lord of peace himself give you peace at all times and in every way. The Lord be with all of you" (2 THESSALONIANS 3:16).

Peace!

" 'IN THIS WORLD
YOU WILL HAVE
TROUBLE.
BUT TAKE HEART!
I HAVE OVERCOME
THE WORLD.' "

JOHN 16:33

GOD WILL ESTABLISH HIS KINGDOM OF PEACE

GOD IS SOVEREIGN, but He is not coercive, manipulative, or excessively controlling. He grieves when we suffer the consequences of our wrong choices, draws us, warns us, pleads with us, confronts us—yet respects the walls we erect between ourselves and Him, seeking to break them down by mutual agreement. We need to place our life in His hands and yield our will to His so He can gain full access to us and assume responsibility for us.

Even so, we won't be exempt from problems. We have an enemy—Satan: thief, devil, liar, adversary, accuser, evil one—whom we must learn to resist and overcome.

How can a sovereign God allow the world to be adversely affected by the devil? We can't answer that completely and certainly not to everyone's satisfaction, but I'm intrigued by a progression of scripture verses. Follow with me, please.

"The earth is the LORD's, and everything in it, the world, and all who live in it" (PSALM 24:1).

That "All things were created by him and for him" (Colossians 1:16)—is easy to accept. However, another verse raises a question:

"The highest heavens belong to the LORD, but the earth he has given to man" (PSALM 115:16).

To man? What an astonishing responsibility God gave to humankind at creation when He said, "Let us make man in our image…and let them rule…over all the earth" (Genesis 1:26).

Now we have a more astonishing verse that says the world is no longer controlled by God, nor by humans:

"We know that we are children of God, and that the whole world is under the control of the evil one" (1 JOHN 5:19).

What happened? The world has gone from God to man to Satan? Is that the reason for wars, accidents, sickness, and catastrophes? Who owns this planet and who controls it?

What would Jesus think of this? Satan appeared to Him one day and made an amazing proposal:

> *"The devil...showed him [Jesus] all the kingdoms of the world and their splendor. 'All this I will give you,' he said, 'if you will bow down and worship me' "*
> (MATTHEW 4:8–9).

Was Satan in a position to negotiate the kingdoms with Jesus? Why didn't Jesus contest Satan's claim to that position? Only after three years, when Jesus was preparing to offer Himself as our Redeemer, did He say:

> *" 'Now is the time for judgment on this world; now the prince of this world will be driven out' "*
> (JOHN 12:31).

Dying for our sins, Jesus embraced a plan that originated with God yet was executed by devil-inspired men who cried: " 'Crucify him! Crucify him!' " (Luke 23:21).

Agonizing on the cross, He cried out words that make it seem as if His efforts had come to nothing and that even the Father who sent Him had given up on Him:

> " *'My God, my God, why have you forsaken me?'* "
> (MARK 15:34).

Yet this moment, that appeared to be the tragic, final defeat of Jesus, was in fact His greatest moment when…

> *"God made him who had no sin to be sin for us, so that in him we might become the righteousness of God"*
> (2 CORINTHIANS 5:21).

Jesus took upon Himself the penalty incurred by our sins and, in so doing, defeated the evil plan of Satan, the usurper of the authority that God had delegated to man in order to rule the world through His created beings:

> *"And having disarmed the powers and authorities, he made a public spectacle of them, triumphing over them by the cross"* (COLOSSIANS 2:15).

Accepting the role for which the Father had prepared Him from eternity past—"the Lamb of God, who takes away the sin of the world" (John 1:29) and "the Lamb that was slain from the creation of the world" (Revelation 13:8)—Jesus paid for our redemption from sin and reclaimed the world from Satan's dominion.

Jesus had come to this world under God's delegated authority, but once He made atonement for sin and was resurrected from the dead, total, absolute authority had been given to Him:

> *"He humbled himself and became obedient to death— even death on a cross! Therefore God exalted him to the highest place and gave him the name that is above every name, that at the name of Jesus every knee should bow, in heaven and on earth and under the earth, and every tongue confess that Jesus Christ is Lord, to the glory of God the Father"* (PHILIPPIANS 2:8–11).

Once God exalted Him and gave Him absolute authority over creation, the resurrected Jesus said to His followers:

> " 'All authority in heaven and on earth has been given to me.
> Therefore go and make disciples of all nations, baptizing them
> in the name of the Father and of the Son and of the Holy Spirit,
> and teaching them to obey everything I have commanded you.
> And surely I am with you always, to the very end of the age' "
>
> (MATTHEW 28:18–20).

Having received authority from the Father, Jesus is King.
He is now extending His kingdom through the church He is
building and sending out, as He was sent by His Father.

His disciples had already started taking the gospel to the
world when Jesus appeared to Paul, who would become history's
greatest spokesperson for Christ. Paul had a vision of what had
to be done and what the final result would be:

> "Then the end will come, when he hands over the kingdom
> to God the Father after he has destroyed all dominion,
> authority and power. For he must reign until he has put all
> his enemies under his feet.… When he has done this, then the
> Son himself will be made subject to him who put everything
> under him, so that God may be all in all"
>
> (1 CORINTHIANS 15:24–25, 28).

After giving this vision to Paul, the resurrected Christ appeared years later to John, who saw a vision of an angel sounding a trumpet while voices in heaven declared:

> " *The kingdom of the world has become the kingdom of our Lord and of his Christ, and he will reign for ever and ever*' " (REVELATION 11:15).

Let's go over it again, reducing the number of words and placing them in an objective, easy-to-follow form. We will see a progression—not a contradiction.

- THE EARTH BELONGS TO GOD THE CREATOR.
- GOD DELEGATES THE EARTH TO MAN TO GOVERN.
- MAN FAILS TO GOVERN THE EARTH AS HE SHOULD.
- THE WORLD COMES UNDER SATAN'S CONTROL.
- SATAN OFFERS IT TO JESUS IN EXCHANGE FOR WORSHIP.
- JESUS REJECTS THE OFFER.
- JESUS BRINGS SALVATION TO US AND DEFEAT TO SATAN BY HIS ATONING DEATH AND RESURRECTION.
- JESUS IS EXALTED TO MAXIMUM AUTHORITY.

- JESUS REIGNS, BUT HIS REIGN MUST BE EXTENDED.
- JESUS CALLS US TO WORK WITH HIM TO WIN THE WORLD.
- THE CHURCH JOINS THE BATTLE THROUGH WORSHIP, SERVICE, PRAYER, EVANGELIZATION, AND DISCIPLESHIP.
- JESUS RETURNS FOR HIS CHURCH AND IN FULL GLORY.
- JESUS JUDGES HUMANITY, CONFERRING ETERNAL LIFE UPON THE SAVED AND ETERNAL PUNISHMENT UPON THE LOST.
- THE KINGDOMS OF THIS WORLD BECOME CHRIST'S AGAIN.
- JESUS OFFERS HIS KINGDOMS TO THE FATHER.
- THE TRIUNE GOD REIGNS OVER ALL FOREVER.
- HIS SAINTS REIGN WITH HIM.

This sequence of events reveals the conflict between the kingdom of God and the kingdom of darkness. Jesus is Lord over all. He will never swerve from His purpose of establishing His eternal kingdom of righteousness. He will let nothing stand in His way. The righteous kingdom that today He proposes will one day be imposed over all.

Peace will reign forever!

NOTES

CHAPTER 2

1. Charles Wesley, "Rejoice, the Lord Is King" (1744).
http://www.cyberhymnal.org/htm/r/e/rejtlord.htm

2. C. Austin Miles, "In the Garden" (1912).
http://www.cyberhymnal.org/htm/i/t/g/itgarden.htm

3. George Foster, "Feelings" (1987).

4. Larry Christenson, *The Renewed Mind* (Minneapolis: Bethany House, 1974, 2002), 26–27.

CHAPTER 3

1. George Foster, *O Poder Restaurador do Perdão* [The Restoring Power of Forgiveness], (Belo Horizonte, Minas Gerais, Brazil: Editora Betânia, 1993), 136.

2. R. T. Kendall, *Total Forgiveness* (London: Hodder and Stoughton, 2001), 4.

CHAPTER 4

1. Edward Mote, "The Solid Rock" (ca.1834).

2. Katharina A. von Schlegel, "Be Still, My Soul" [Stille, Meine Wille, dein Jesus Hilft Siegen], (1752). Translated from German to English by Jane L. Borthwick in *Hymns from the Land of Luther* (1855).

3. Rick Warren, *The Purpose-Driven Life* (Grand Rapids: Zondervan, 2002), 186.

CHAPTER 5

1. Joseph Scriven, "What a Friend We Have in Jesus" (1855).
2. Andrew Murray, *Teach Us to Pray* (Minneapolis, Bethany House, 1981, 2002), 12.
3. George Foster, "Do You Hear My Prayer?" (1994).
4. Scriven, "What a Friend."

CHAPTER 7

1. William Backus, *Telling Yourself the Truth* (Minneapolis: Bethany House, 1980, 1981, 2000), introduction.

CHAPTER 9

1. Oswald Chambers, ed. James G. Reimann, *My Utmost for His Highest* (Grand Rapids: Discovery House Publishers, 1996), August 26.
2. Lareau Lindquist, *Encouragement: The Online Magazine* (Rockford: Barnabas International, 2002). http://barnabas.org/magazine.php